MEMORY CARDS

PORTRAITS FROM A RURAL JOURNEY

MICHAEL K. BRANTLEY

ISBN: 978-1-61296-536-9

PUBLISHED BY BLACK ROSE WRITING

www.blackrosewriting.com

Printed in the United States of America

Suggested retail price $15.95

Memory Cards is printed in Adobe Garamond Pro

For Holly, Kent and Lowell

ACKNOWLEDGMENTS

There are countless people who made this book happen, and I know if I try to list them all, I will surely leave someone out. However, my conscience requires me to name at least a few key folks.

Black Rose Writing is responsible for this book being in your hands, having taken the risk to publish a new author. It is nice to work with a publisher who contacts me personally, and offers clear expectations as well as support.

Jim McKean is at once one of the finest writers and poets I've ever known, and one of the best men I've ever had the pleasure to know. At the very least, he has a high threshold of pain and patience, guiding so much of this book with an uncanny insight, through countless reads, while telling me what I needed to hear when I needed to hear it. His wise counsel runs through my head with everything I write now. I'm proud to call him teacher, mentor and most importantly, friend. Read his work.

Accomplished authors Emily Fox-Gordon and Jon Pineda were adept at constantly challenging me and putting me outside my comfort zone, making me look at my work from a different angle. They stuck with me even in my most "hard-headed" moments. I owe them for all they've shared.

ECU Professor Alex Albright gets a nod for starting this project with a 300-word assignment that eventually morphed into a 65,000-word book. He is a master of creative nonfiction. I still have all the notes from his classes.

I can't think of a more unlikely writing partnership than with my best bud Ann Fitzmaurice. We survived an MFA program even though we read every single word each of us wrote. Her questions, goading, editing and suggestions were always kind and sincere, and she is not just a fine writer, but a superb editor.

I saved them for last, but they are certainly not least: my family. My mama, Margie Brantley, was the first supporter of my writing, and I can't put into words how important it was to have that growing up. My children, who are featured in various roles in this book, gave up time with their daddy so he could write, but they also provided inspiration and material. As for my wife, Kristi, I don't know where to start or finish. I love her more every day. Her unwavering support from the minute I mentioned "grad school," to the countless reads and edits, to always picking me up when I needed it, I'll have to just say "Thank you."

—*Michael K. Brantley*

Some of these chapters appeared in one form or another in the following journals:

"Barbecue with Kent," *Wordriver* and *The Smoking Poet*; "The Monkey on My Back," *The Dunes Review*; "Paid by the Inch," *Biostories*; "Small Game," *Stymie*; "Tea Cookies," *Vine Leaves Literary Journal*; "The Indian Hole," *Revolution House*; "Rationed," *The Sandy River Review*; "Memory Cards," *The Magnolia Review*; "Me and John and Gus and Hairy," *The Cobalt Review*; "Let Me Call My Sales Manager," *Prime Number Magazine*; and "Homecoming," *The First Day*.

Memory Cards

Contents

1

Barbecue with Kent

We pull into the restaurant parking lot on a late afternoon that looks more like a cold, bleak, Monday in February than a Friday afternoon in mid-September. However, as we step out of my Honda Civic, we are met by a combination of drizzling rain and mugginess — the feeling that a warm, wet blanket had been tossed around our necks. Summers in North Carolina do not yield easily to the next season.

The parking lot is a pockmarked jumble of black asphalt with utility poles located in the most awkward of places. I haven't visited this joint in a long time, and I find myself wondering why anyone would place utility poles right in the middle of traffic lanes and parking spaces. Then I remember that the highway has meandered since the restaurant's first day of business, shortly after the end of World War II. The restaurant still appears as it did when I was a child — a large, long, white building with a single sign mounted on the roof displaying the name of the original proprietor in blue-black letters: Parker's Barbecue.

A funny thing about Parker's is how the parking lot has its own neatly divided demographics. In front of the main entrance, where the dine-in area is located, the spaces are filled with minivans, station wagons, immaculate pickup trucks and long, American-made sedans — the crowd made up of retirees and middle-aged farmers, mostly. Those are the early birds, folks who roll in starting around 4 p.m. The takeout parks, around to the side, are a bit more egalitarian: RVs, rust buckets, giant, muddy pickup trucks and small foreign-made hatchbacks — these drivers love the same food, but lack either the means or the time to sit down for a meal inside.

The name Parker's Barbecue says it all. For folks from eastern North Carolina, no other qualifier is needed. They know exactly what is cooked, served and packaged at a frenetic pace seven days a week, all day long — barbecue. Barbecue is not a verb, it is not a noun that needs an adjective denoting what animal the meat comes from (pig), it is not an event. Its authenticity is regional, no different than gumbo is to Louisiana, brisket is to Texas, cheese steaks are to Philadelphia or bagels are to New York City.

• • •

Parker's, on a blighted stretch of U.S. Highway 301 in Wilson, has changed little in the generations that have passed since it opened the doors shortly after World War II. Despite living so close to such a fine establishment, our family of five rarely dines on barbecue. I grew up on the stuff – finely chopped pork shoulder, seasoned with vinegar and crushed red pepper; nearly pureed slaw made with a heavy hand of celery salt, mustard and sugar; Brunswick stew; boiled white potatoes; cornbread sticks; and of course, hushpuppies. Fried chicken fit to rival the best anyone's mama has put on the table, is usually a side dish, as is barbecued chicken, cooked right alongside the pig. The menu is as plain as the building. It should also be noted that the sweeter the ice tea is at a barbecue joint, the better the food will be. A person served unsweetened tea should pay for the drinks and leave immediately. The tea at Parker's is very sweet.

When I was a child in the late 1970s and early 1980s, we got most of our food off the family farm. For the occasional treat, and to give my mama a break from her usual routine of cooking three meals a day, my parents took my brothers and sisters and me out for a family meal at Parker's. We sat at long tables covered in white butcher paper, and ate food off brown plastic cafeteria-style plates loaded with barbecue and the trimmings. My siblings always got a combination, with fried chicken and barbecue sharing the meat space on the plate, along with potatoes and slaw, the natural companion to pork. For me, barbecue was a delicacy, and I wasn't about to sacrifice half my share for a drumstick or wing; double slaw and cornbread was all I needed for accompaniment, until I got older and developed a taste for Brunswick stew. Daddy's plate always seemed piled a little higher than the others, Mama's a little more modest.

Young boys from the local high schools or Atlantic Christian College waited the tables. Each was decked out in a white shirt, white pants, a white apron and a white paper hat. Those boys practically ran from the kitchen to the tables, refilling drinks and doing all the bus work, clattering red tumblers, trays, chicken bones, napkins and silverware into big plastic tubs. A generation ago, a single plate of more food than a normal adult should eat in one sitting could be had for a couple of dollars, just right for my folks' budget, which was strictly based on the cash in Daddy's well-worn, black leather wallet.

• • •

My middle son, age six, loves to go places he's never been, especially if those places are somehow connected to my childhood. As we found a parking space near the side entrance at Parker's, between a well-worn dingy white Chevy custom van with blue pinstripes and a massive black Z-71 truck, I told him we'd be getting takeout, having just come from a rain-shortened youth soccer practice.

He always peppers me with questions, and today is no different. This section of Wilson is long past its heyday, now that I-95 has supplanted the old highway as the major artery leading north-south, the halfway mark between New York and Florida. Highway 301 was once bustling with neon-lit motels, restaurants, gas stations and the city fairgrounds across the street. It looks like 1962 just packed up one day and left. Kent wanted to know why everything looked so old and broken. The area is flat, and many of the pine trees that added life and color were thinned first by Hurricane Floyd back in 1999 and then by two rounds of tornadoes the past three years. It is hard to tell if some of the single-story "motor courts" are still open. One is occupied by a Chinese restaurant with no cars on the lot at the dinner hour, just a lonely red OPEN sign on the office door. Another houses a Mexican grocery, while the neighboring establishment that looks right out of a postcard from Highway 66, is seedy-looking enough to be doing trade of a different kind. Almost all of the buildings need renovation or demolition, but are unlikely to get either.

We work our way towards the takeout annex, which is tucked around the north side of the restaurant, away from the high traffic goings-on at the front door to the dining area. Tall, skinny and athletic, my orange-haired boy — he doesn't like to be called a redhead — sticks close to me. The backside of Parker's doesn't have much curb appeal and old, run-down storage buildings with flaking paint are surrounded by knee-high grass and weeds. Crates, pallets, delivery boxes and miscellaneous debris lay scattered in the back of the building. Kent asks if I am sure we're going the right way. We walk up an old-style ramp with indoor-outdoor carpeting, open the screen door and step back in time.

• • •

I guess my generation, the one known as X, started the breakup with restaurants like Parker's. Diets have changed. Farmers and blue-collar workers had long days of physical labor to help offset what would be considered a high-calorie, high-cholesterol lunch today. Travelers and buyers from what was once the world's largest tobacco market knew the places they could count on for good, cheap food to get them through the day.

Maybe barbecue is the forerunner to today's fast food, only it doesn't come packed with artificial fillers and loaded with additives and preservatives.

Where there were once barbecue places and greasy spoons on every street corner of towns across the eastern part of the state, there are now Mexican and Chinese restaurants. These places provide no healthier alternative for the 18-to-35-year-old working professionals, they are just trendier. There has been essentially a patron-cide for an entire segment of the population. I suspect General Tso's Chicken, or carnitas, will keep heart bypass doctors just as busy in the coming years as the places serving grilled pig doused with vinegar.

• • •

We walk across an old, but clean gray-painted concrete floor and stand in a line that is nearly ten deep with customers, cooled by a single, ancient ceiling fan. A few stray flies work the room. I groan to myself, fearing a long wait and a soon-to-be-impatient first grader. But two young men, probably still in their teens, work the register with precision. They turn their ears towards the customer, scribble orders on a stubbed pad, ring up totals, collect cash, give change and pass the details to a waiting crewmember. Another dozen boys work an assembly line in the background, tightly packing barbecue, vegetables and trimmings into plastic containers, and then double-bagging each order. McDonald's wishes they could turn orders that fast. The workers still wear the white aprons, shirts and paper hats.

The line moves quickly and suddenly I realize I have no idea what I'm going to order and how much I need. The wall menu is the type you see at high school concession stands, featuring a soft drink company's logo and sporting blue plastic snap-on letters. I'm lost on quantities. Kent tells me to be sure to get him some cornsticks, he would really like one, he's never had one, and by the way, what are they? He points out we should get chicken as well, as he watches a worker use metal tongs to dump large crispy wings and legs, one after another into a large bag, until it is almost full, then he tops it with cornsticks. Kent is practically licking his lips. Fried chicken is his favorite.

There is no place for debit cards in this world, so I check the cash in my wallet and order accordingly. My transaction and the filling of my order are almost instantaneous, and the bag is warm to the touch. We excuse ourselves through the mass of people who have entered the building since we arrived and emerge from the past to find the rain has stopped, and in its place a cool breeze greets us. Kent says he hopes I got enough food, he's starving.

• • •

We spend most of the 30-minute, back roads drive home talking about what Parker's was like when I was a kid. I tell him about how his aunts and uncles, all a decade or more my senior, laughed and cut-up at the table, while his Mammy answered my endless questions, like I do for him now. I tell him how good the food was then, and how we only went out to eat a few times a year and that it was usually a big deal, a much different lifestyle than his. He asks why we don't ever go now, and that sometime, he'd like to go in and sit down like I used to do. I'm tempted to dig into the bag and fish out two cornsticks — cigar-shaped, thin strips of cornmeal, deep-fried to a crispy crust— and pass one to Kent to try. I decide against it. The aroma of all the good things we'll have for supper heightens our anticipation, and I wonder if my kids will enjoy the food the way I did at their age. My question is answered shortly after we walk into the kitchen at home. His older sister and younger brother meet us at the counter, my wife trailing behind, all drawn to the aroma of grilled pork, pepper, cornsticks, chicken and stew.

We have plastic trays at home, but the not the generic variety of my childhood; these feature cartoon characters and superheroes. The kids bounce impatiently in their chairs as the food is piled in front of them, and the next thirty minutes is silent except for the smacking and finger-licking and calls for more. The taste is just as I remembered it: the cool sweetness of the slaw a perfect counterpunch to the saltiness of the vinegar drenched meat and the tanginess of the rich, spicy, tomato-based Brunswick stew, made for dipping the crunchy slabs of cornmeal into. It will take two more well-savored meals to clean up the leftover barbecue, slaw and Brunswick stew. The chicken and cornsticks never had a chance.

Food is a tie that binds us, and regional foods are at risk for losing their authenticity at the hands of a society demanding fast, bland, boring sameness. No one comes home for a Big Mac or MSG-laden rice. When locals who have moved away from here come back to visit, a barbecue place is one of their main priorities— either for a meal or to take some back home, to work those great memories back into their lives. Loyalties to barbecue establishments create friendly rivalries that are second only to college basketball in North Carolina.

We could have chopped pork just about anytime based on price and proximity, but rarely do. I realized after that night of Parker's that I have become one of the people I complain about — those who have abandoned the institutions that ought to be saved. Places like Parker's, places with personalities, define and distinguish communities and regions. Hectic lifestyles and changing interests took us down other pathways, much the way childhood buddies drift apart. My complicity in abandoning an old family favorite, albeit unintentional, makes me feel somewhat hypocritical. After all, my future grandchildren ought not be deprived of a place so special and nostalgic in my memory, and now, just maybe, also in Kent's.

• • •

2

The Monkey on My Back

The summer I went to the field the first time, Daddy rented part of his allotment to another farmer and we had our smallest crop ever. He had started working as an office manager for a welding supply company in Rocky Mount, and when the crop was in and had been sold, he and Mama made an announcement at supper one night.

"We're not going to farm anymore," they said.

My brothers and sisters were devastated. Mama seemed sad. To this day, they talk about how awful the news was, even though they suspected it was coming. It was all I could do to keep from shouting with joy. I've always said that was the happiest day of my childhood, the day I knew I wouldn't have to go to the fields again.

• • •

We were priming tobacco, and it was my first season in the rows — bending, snapping the wide, green, pungent leaves, tucking them under our arms. When loaded down, we quick-stepped to the trailer and stacked the load. My brothers Bill and Jimmy, at 10 and 15 years older (I was nine), were much more skilled than me, and had no trouble keeping up with the tractor, which plodded along under the guidance of Daddy.

After years of child's jobs at the barns, I finally was out with the men. I didn't want to get teased by my brothers and their friends, and I didn't want to get yelled at by Daddy. We were near the end of the season, and this was the last field to be harvested.

What really had me worried as the reality of the work settled in, though, was the possibility of "getting the monkey on my back." That was something you could never get away from, never live down, never put behind you; it meant you couldn't handle the job, the result being you got sick right there in the field. Tobacco has an odor that pierces the nostrils, sickly sweet, but sour at the same time; a scent so strong it quickly puts a nauseating, metallic taste on the back of your throat. The stickiness, known as gum, leaves a black residue on a worker's hands, and burns if it accidentally touches eyes, lips or open cuts. Barning tobacco was tough work. It was brutal in August when North Carolina becomes a still-air firepots. No breeze, nothing to keep the gnats away, the sun straight overhead, punishing all those under it. I felt the moisture being drawn out of me, through my pores, and into the air, adding to the humidity and misery of the afternoon.

• • •

A typical day during tobacco season started before first light. After Mama cooked a full breakfast for the family — my sisters Jane and Carol worked as well — everyone headed out the door for their prep tasks. The women got the looper ready, my brothers made sure the tractor was gassed and the tobacco trucks (wagons) were hitched.

I rode with my dad down to Pace's store, just a couple of miles away. I had to remember to wear shoes, because instead of a gravel or dirt parking lot, Pace's was covered with metal soft drink bottle caps. The store was like an old barn, cool and dark and musty, with just one front window and a screen door, and lit with bare light bulbs hanging straight down from black cords. Waist-high, silver metal Pepsi and Coca-Cola coolers, the kind with the solid sliding door tops, lined the walls, offering a blast of stale, but frigid air to the face when opened. Wooden crates stacked on their sides were set up for returns, and bottle openers were nailed to several places on the wall. Oversize glass cookie jars were filled with small bags of salted peanuts, which many folks poured into a cold Pepsi as a treat. Pork n' Beans, Vienna Sausages and Potted Meat were all grouped together, as the proprietor knew his market.

Mr. Pace, a large man, was always behind the counter, and he'd punch up Daddy's totals on the crank cash register — a crate of glass bottle Coca-Colas, Mountain Dews, Pepsis, Grape Nehis, and my favorite, Orange Crush; a box of Nabs and a couple of boxes of honey buns and Moon Pies or Big Towns for morning break time. Daddy dropped the tailgate, filled up a cooler or old wash tub with ice, and then I shoved the drinks in one at the time. On the way home, we'd pick up any extra help we might need for the day.

By the time we got back to the house, the rusty Texaco thermometer nailed to a post in the barnyard would already be pushing towards the 80s. Daddy parked the truck under a shade tree in the yard, climbed up on the tractor, and the field workers hopped on the trailer to ride out to the fields. I stood and watched as the tractor made its way down the path and meadow strip, and waded into a sea of wide, green leaves, that in just a few months would head down the road to Wilson to be sold. It was physically demanding work, the only kind my parents had ever known. My brothers and sisters didn't seem to mind it, enjoyed being outdoors, and considered farm life something they might do for a living, while I dreamed of other things.

• • •

We grew all of our vegetables, eating fresh from a huge garden all summer, and canning and preserving for the winter. New potatoes, sweet potatoes, corn, snaps and greens were all in plentiful supply. Overage was sold to local grocery stores or at the farmers markets. Mama never bought a vegetable in a store until she was in her 60s. We had cows and hogs, most of which were sold, but a few were held out for personal use. Usually one of the coldest days of winter was chosen for an all-day event of slaughtering and processing an animal, dividing cuts of meat, hanging hams to cure, making sausage, and ending with a big meal and freezer full of pork or beef to last a year.

But tobacco was the cash crop. It paid for utilities, clothes, gas and all the other necessities we couldn't produce. There was relatively little immigrant labor in those days, and those workers mostly labored on the large farms that provided "camps" — a nice word for hovels — for housing. Families of usually four to eight people would be crammed into two room, concrete block houses, which came four or five to a unit, usually without running water. Outhouses, portajohns, and wells with spigots served the camp's needs, and of course, these most basic of shelters were charged against wages earned in the field. When we rode by these places, I saw the migrant families and thought how miserable and sad they looked, and wondered if things were any different for them when in the fall they headed to Florida and Texas for winter work. To get our crop in, we relied on family, neighbors, friends, young and old, black and white, anyone willing to put in a full day's work for cash money.

Tobacco is harvested over a couple of months in the summer, but there was a lot to be done to get it from plant bed to curing barn to auction. We planted our seeds right after New Year's Day, sown closely together for warmth. Mama always cooked hog jowls and black-eyed peas for good luck, because an old wives' tale used to say that you'd make a dollar for every pea you ate on the first day of the year. Though they haven't grown tobacco in over 30 years, my parents still eat this meal on January 1 every year; I'm still invited, but always pass.

The soil in a patch of field was hand raked with hoes and picked clean of weeds. Clear plastic was used to cover the seeds, allowing sunlight in, while keeping the cold weather from killing the seedlings. The plants grew and started pushing the plastic up, which we took off after the last killing frost had passed. The plants were carefully dug up, and transplanted in April. We had a three-seat transplanter that attached to the old Farmall tractor. The hopper was filled with plants, and riders dropped them one-by-one onto a track that would stick the plants in the ground. If any plants died or were crushed, my brothers used rounded wooden stobs called tobacco pegs to dig a new hole and replace the plant. Fields were checked everyday to see if replacements were needed, as every space was too valuable to leave unfilled — the government set strict acreage allotments on what a farmer could grow, so yields had to be maximized.

By June, it was time to sucker, or top the tobacco, which was done by hand. When a tobacco plant gets about shoulder high on an average sized man, purple-pink and white flowers sprout from the top. These have to be broken off for the plant to fully develop. I never understood the science of it, but the tobacco plant would somehow takeoff, and the leaves fanned out and added weight once this was done. Weight and better looking leaves meant more money at sale time in August and September. A farmer just needs timely rain, no hail, and lots of heat for a good crop. Eastern North Carolina is always good for at least two out of three.

• • •

Every four or five rows in a tobacco field, we left a wide row open, wide enough to drive the tractor. The space between rows of plants was very tight, with the leaves reaching across to block the way of the primer. Primers started low on the plant, just above the mounded soil, reached in, snapped the stem from the stalk in one twist, sort of like a baseball swing in reverse. A primer worked about one-third to one-fourth of each plant on each pass through a field; it took several days of working a field to completely strip a stalk, so the upper leaves could continue to grow.

Workers were expected to keep up with the tractor and trailer. Tobacco plants are tough and stringy, and often hid wasps or spiders or worms or other stinging insects. The lower hanging leaves were the biggest and heaviest, but it was tough stooping down in the heat and humidity, sweat and salt running into the mouth and nose, each breath stifled by the stinging smell of the plants. It was a smell that stayed in the nostrils, lingering, and it singed my throat. The black gum worked its way into the creases and crevices of hands and it burned. Tobacco gum didn't come off easy, sometimes not at all, and it stained hands for the whole summer.

On those hot days in July and August, a real fear was getting the monkey on your back. After bending up and down those rows for an hour or so, clothes soaked first with dew from the leaves in the morning, and then from sweat, a man not used to the work could get an odd feeling. Bend, snap, crouch forward, bend, snap, hustle to trailer, drop the leaves, back down, inhale. My brothers said you could see it coming. The victim might look flush, then dizzy, and he'd feel like a monkey had climbed on his back, one arm around his neck, the other swinging and pulling. Some could fight the feeling off, but for many, the nausea was too much, and they would get sick right there in the row, or worse, bolt out of the field for all to see, adding to sickness with embarrassment.

• • •

When a trailer was full, Daddy took it to the barnyard. We had two barns, about fifty feet apart, with a tin-covered shelter connecting them. The trailer was unhitched and moved directly behind the women, who ran the gas-powered looper — a long, metal conveyor belt on wheels with one end extending into an open barn door. Mama and my sisters worked behind the looper, laying down leaves in even bunches. After a layer was done, my job was to push a wooden 2x2-inch tobacco stick up against metal pegs that served as guides. Once the stick was down, another layer of leaves was added, and then the leaves and stick passed under what amounted to a large sewing machine, which stitched the leaves onto the stick. The stick rode the belt to the barn entrance for hanging.

Our barns were wood, with tin siding and brick and concrete foundations, three stories high, with rafters spaced out to the ceiling. At the start of the day, one man climbed to the top rafter, one man to the middle and one stood on the dirt floor to pass the sticks up. The barn was packed half full by lunch, when we'd break and Mama went in to fix the family something to eat, while the workers sat under a tree with their lunch boxes. Some of them ate quickly to get a nap in before the rest of the afternoon was used to finish filling the barn. By the end of the day, the barn was full of leaf, ready to be cured.

Metal burners were set up across the floor of the barn and lit, minipots hanging by rusted chains from what looked like a rounded end table. My dad got up during the night to go check on them, to make sure all the pots were firing and that nothing had fallen onto a burner that would cause a fire. As the tobacco started curing, as bad as those leaves had smelled that afternoon in the field, the aroma that filled the air was altogether different. That time of year, you could go anywhere in Nash County and smell that smell. It was sweet and musky, not the smell of something burning, and certainly not the smell of someone puffing a cigarette or a pipe or a cigar. It was the smell of a farm.

The next day, the cycle started again.

Both barns being full gave a few days break from the field. As each barn cured out, the leaves were dumped and packed in burlap sheets. When the stalks were completely stripped, the packhouse was full of bundles of beautiful, dry, golden leaf ready for market. As sale time got closer, the mood became lighter around the farm, and plans were made for the end of season trip to White Lake for vacation, and a week or so after that, to Raleigh for school clothes and supplies.

Daddy checked the paper, listened to the radio and watched the TV to decide when the best time was to load up the truck and trailer and head to one of the sales in Wilson, the largest tobacco market in the world, just 30 minutes southeast down the road. The bundles would be laid out with the best, prettiest leaves on top at places like Liberty

Warehouse or Bright Leaf Warehouse, as buyers from all the major processing companies would follow the auctioneer, bidding and buying in a flurry of rhythmic chants and hand signals only those in the know could understand. From there, the leaf would go on to Durham, Winston-Salem or Richmond to be made into cigarettes or chew or snuff or other products to be shipped all over the universe, of which North Carolina was the center. His bundles sold, Daddy was off to the cashier's office to stand in line and wait for a crisp, blue check to be punched out of a hand-cranked device, showing in red and black dots just how much our labors and luck were worth that year.

• • •

After getting out of the tobacco growing business, things went well for the next year or two. Soon enough, Daddy got rid of the cows and hogs. We still had the large garden, but tomatoes, corn, peppers, beans, peas and sweet potatoes were not as demanding as tobacco. My folks remodeled the house, I got a window unit air conditioner and a six-inch black and white hand-me-down television for my room. My brothers and sisters all got married and moved out, leaving me as an only child as I approached the beginning of my teenage years.

However, my joy was short-lived. I came home from school one rainy day to find out that my brother, with Daddy's help, had decided to put in a commercial hog operation. While the farm was as modern as the 1980s had to offer, they still needed someone to feed, inoculate pigs and work the business end of a shovel and water hose. That was my new part time job, for which I would be paid $1.50 an hour.

A new routine started for me after school. I spent a couple of hours doing hard, smelly work before I was allowed to come home and shoot basketball the rest of the afternoon. Hogs like mud and manure, and even though temperatures were regulated with fans and curtains, the heat and the smell would get up my nose and I could not get rid of it. Sometimes, after working and then playing ball, I'd take two showers, but I could still smell manure. Mama laughed and said it was all in my head.

In the days before hog farmers signed production contracts with processors, hog farming was a risky business. A couple of years in, I began to sense something wasn't quite right, and there seemed to be tension in the house. Mama was stressed. One afternoon, we rode over to the homeplace, the land near our house where my grandfather had grown up, and his family before him, land my daddy had inherited. Not much was said in the pickup, between Daddy, Mama and me. I was bored, and they were unusually quiet.

About two weeks later, my parents sold that property to a large-scale farmer. Staggering debt had been piled up on the hog farm. Savings accounts were wiped out. There would be no rental income for retirement. They never talked about the problem openly in front of me, but I put pieces together here and there about what happened. Mama told me years later that she and Daddy had figured a way out, but the loan officer at the farm credit agency would not give them an additional week to make arrangements, demanding immediate payment or foreclosure. More than thirty years later, when I see a billboard for that institution, I still feel the anger flush in my cheeks.

The impact of these problems touched me a few years later when I was in high school and started applying to colleges. With a schedule of honors classes and promises heaped on by teachers and guidance counselors, I had a long list of schools to examine for my ticket off the farm. Until it came time to put those forms in the mail.

"We need to talk about school," Mama said, right in the middle of an excited monologue I had rattled off about Chapel Hill or Greenville or Raleigh. "We're going to do all we can, we'll borrow the money if we can, but you might have to wait a year to go. But hopefully, you'll be able to go somewhere."

I remember that day well, where I was standing in the living room, where Mama was standing, the defeated look on her face. This was not the way it was supposed to be, for her or me. It was not the way things had been promised, not the way things happened for students with solid (if not spectacular) SAT scores who had been told they could do anything they wanted. The monkey was on my back, with one arm around my neck, swinging, and pulling with the other arm, the nausea rising inside me.

• • •

I worked part time jobs at newspapers, saved almost every dime I made and ended up applying to two schools. At the last minute, Barton College, in Wilson, sweetened the pot with some scholarships and grants. I commuted and saved even more.

While I didn't get off the land, I did get off the farm, got a degree and a wife. I ended up going to the other school, East Carolina, twenty years later, for a master's degree in English.

As a wedding present, Kristi and I were given a corner on the farm to build a home and start a family. For 15 years, we did nothing farm related. But, as homesteading and whole foods movements gained traction we considered how we wanted to raise our kids, what we wanted them putting into their bodies and the mass-market food sources. We bought some laying hens to free range, and planted blueberries, blackberries, fig trees and even a few vegetables. About a year after that, I fenced in the edge of the overgrown fields and woods and made a pasture for dairy goats. We have a beehive. After spending a lifetime of running from the farm, we started a micro-farm. It is not the farm my parents had, it is one of our own making.

We get eggs and milk, and make goat cheese and soap. The berries are so sweet, we rarely end up with any to share or sell. Sometimes I find myself just standing in the pasture, rubbing the goats' heads after I feed them. There is a comfort to watching them eat and grow, and help manage the land, as well as make all of our fertilizer.

MEMORY CARDS

I overheard one of my sisters talking to someone at a family function about a year ago. "I never thought I'd see Michael, of all people, ever farm." None of my siblings, the ones who sat at the table that night 30-some years ago, upset and sad that the farm life was over, even has so much as a garden box today. Only I do, as I look over my shoulder and keep an eye out for the next monkey.

• • •

3

Paid by the Inch

I remember exactly where I was sitting — the next to last seat, last row, just in front of the door — when the Bantam rooster who taught our journalism class perched on the corner of his desk, and began to squawk about his disappointment with our efforts on the forthcoming first issue of the student newspaper.

What a load of garbage, he said. Did anybody listen to directions? Do you want to be the class who kills *The Phoenix*? Mr. Transou was new to the school, and I think he even compared the pieces on his desk to dog turds.

Then Transou did the unthinkable. He said let's read some of this crap. And he started reaching for manuscripts from his pile. There were grumbles as he shot down one piece after the other, mostly making the point that no one had put any effort into the assignment. I waited for my turn. People were doodling on notebooks, looking at the clock, hoping for a fire drill or bomb threat or something that would save us all. I felt alone in my first year at the senior high school, in my first period class. Sporting a bowl haircut, a disproportioned body I was trying to grow into and Coke-bottle glasses, I knew just one person in class — a girl I'd had a crush on since seventh grade.

Everyone else was a junior or senior, mostly popular students. We had a couple of blonde cheerleaders, a couple of athletes, a handful of slackers, and some "popular girls." Naïve as one could get in the mid-1980s, I didn't realize that Journalism was a crip course.

Now, Transou said, after about seven or eight pieces, listen to this one. "So, you think you know sports, huh?" As he rolled the first line of my story off his lips, I looked down and cringed. What does that make you think, he asked. No one answered.

I'll tell you what it makes me think, he said. It makes me want to read more. That's a lead. And the worst part is, he continued, is I've got a roomful of seniors in here and you let a dad-blame sophomore show you all up. That guy right there, he said. I looked up just in time to see him point my paper back at me.

Deep down, I was excited. I had spent some time on the work, banging away on a typewriter, not really knowing what I was doing. I felt the laser-like burn of eyes cast my way, eyes showing resentment and scorn. I saw what I would later come to appreciate and know as Mr. Transou's devilish grin —a sort of sideways, sarcastic twist of the mouth, like a poker tell, which preceded wrath, a smart aleck comeback or a slash to cut someone down to size. He pushed his glasses up on his nose, flipped his black mop of hair and said it: Brantley's going to be our sports editor. The teacher had hung a bull's-eye on me, giving a bottom-feeding underclassman an editorial position.

The girl I had the crush on reached across the aisle and touched my arm. Good job, Mikey, she said. I no longer cared who else in the room hated me.

• • •

Maybe it's therapeutic, maybe it's egotistical, maybe it is just angst. Dylan Thomas gave it a good turn in "In My Craft or Sullen Art," when he compared writing to two frustrated lovers, and mentioned that he doesn't write for money or fame or ambition or for a certain class. He writes for the people who won't even read his work: "...But for the lovers, their arms/Round the griefs of the ages/Who pay no praise or wages/Nor heed my craft or art."

A colleague once asked me if all writers were damaged. Maybe. I think my story is more about "labour by singing light," only in my version, I'm more like a clumsy plumber in a jumbled crawl space trying to use McKenna's left-handed monkey wrench — I keep banging my knuckles against all the pipes.

There is deep satisfaction to making something where nothing existed, not even raw material. It is no different than the feeling a maker of fine guitars has when he puts that last coat of varnish over the headstock adorned with his name; the pride of the furniture maker who burns his mark into the underside of a cherry dinette; or the artist as he stands back and admires his work before at last blessing it with a signature. Artists don't make a career choice, they respond to a calling, sometimes with only a byline and two contributor's copies to serve as compensation.

• • •

Within a couple of weeks of being named sports editor and getting my first two articles published in the high school newspaper, I became a professional writer. *The Nashville Graphic* needed a part-time sportswriter — stringers, they were called — to cover my high school. The publisher had seen my stories and she had a paying job for me if I wanted it. The job paid by the inch, she said. Stringers started at 50 cents per column inch of copy published. I wasn't sure how much money this would amount to, but I knew being paid to watch sports beat shoveling manure for the $2 an hour I was making on my family's hog farm. There was just one hitch. I hadn't yet become eligible for driver's ed. I asked the publisher if I could call her back, once I checked with my folks about transportation.

There was a pause on the other end of the phone. "Michael, are you telling me you aren't old enough to drive?" the publisher asked.

"Yes ma'am."

She laughed. "You talk to your folks and call me back."

So, for six months, Mama dropped me off at basketball and baseball games, and later at town hall meetings, county commissioner meetings, election nights and other events important to community newspapers.

I had great editors at the *Graphic*. The first one was straight-laced, by the book, and taught me all the rules. He taught me how to "write tight," and take notes in a way that would allow the stories to be quickly constructed. He toughened my skin, sharpened my writing (the fewer words the better) and insisted on unbiased reporting.

My next editor at the paper was more of the artistic type. He taught me to add color, to appeal to the senses, to think beyond the plays, to put readers in the action. I got an education, eventually worked in every department at the newspaper, and earned enough money to buy a wrecked '84 Chevette. I was soaked deeply in printer's ink.

• • •

My experience got me freelance work in college covering sports for the Raleigh *News & Observer*. It was good work, I got plum assignments in the eastern half of North Carolina, especially during football season, and it kept me in gas money and books. There was something wonderful about working a game, and just six hours later picking up a copy of the paper and seeing my story in the sports section. It was akin to seeing a black and white print come to life in a darkroom developing tray. In the early 1990s, there were no laptops and no smartphones, so I had to call my stories in from the nearest pay phone I could find after a game. Some nights, there was no time to write out copy. The night editor, an old school reporter I had grown up reading, had me compose my pieces verbally, straight from the notes, encouraging me as I rattled off paragraphs in the parking lots of country stores, gas stations and greasy spoons that had closed for the night.

After college, I worked as editor of a local newspaper and then rejoined *The Nashville Graphic*. But as much as I loved the work, I started considering the future. I was newly married and we wanted to start a family at some point and have some stability. The news business is all about movement. To get ahead, you have to keep stepping up the ladder, moving and hustling and working long hours. I started to realize that very few of my colleagues in the industry stayed married, and an alarming number had drinking problems. I soon left for a job in public relations.

It didn't take long to miss writing. I started hunting freelance work, first with a regional business magazine, then a national sports magazine, a farm publication and a bluegrass music monthly. Just as I was considering jumping into freelancing fulltime, a friend wanted to know if I was interested in purchasing his photography business. I would still be able to tell stories, just with images, not words. My notes and journals went into the bottom drawer of my desk for almost two decades. So did my calling.

• • •

In early 2012, I walked across a stage at East Carolina University and took a piece of paper that represented a Master of Arts in English. It was the end of a whirlwind year and a half that began when I decided I'd had enough of Photoshopping, crying babies, late night alcohol-fueled wedding receptions, a tanking economy and more than a few difficult customers. At 41, it seemed crazy to my family and friends for me to try to start over, especially after 17 years of running my own business. To me, it seemed long overdue. It was like the scene in "Forrest Gump" where Forrest runs across the country for years and then decides one day that he doesn't want to run anymore, so he stops.

I was going to back to writing, the thing I was called to do. But I knew I needed more.

Two weeks after finishing my degree, I dropped my bags into a dorm room at Queens University of Charlotte, to begin coursework on an MFA in Creative Writing. It is strange, but liberating when you stop denying who you are.

• • •

Books were important at my house growing up. Every night, Mama read to me — Dr. Seuss, Curious George, Sunny Books and all sorts of children's literature anthologies. Of course, there weren't a whole lot of alternatives after the work on the farm was done. Our tiny black and white television picked up only three channels — four if the weather was just right —and all my brothers and sisters were grown.

Though we lived on a tight, cash-only budget, my parents subscribed to the *News & Observer*. They read every page of it every day. There was one columnist who was a family favorite. Dennis Rogers hit every back road in the state for decades, going into towns and finding stories to fill his space five days a week. Rogers wrote about dive bars, veterans, upstanding citizens, crooks, hangings, legends, good old boys, and women down on their luck. His work was sometimes funny, sometimes gritty, but always authentic. He created vivid scenes. I learned that everyone or every place has a story, it just takes a writer to find it and make it ready to be read. My family would talk about Rogers' pieces, and I was motivated to read so I would not be left out of the conversation.

I devoured books like a stray dog might attack a plate of table scraps. Whenever I had questions, my parents would tell me to "go look it up," in the set of World Book Encyclopedias so old it didn't have any mention of the Vietnam War. I read biographies of the Founding Fathers, moved on to the Hardy Boys, American history, spy novels by Ian Fleming, Ellery Queen, and *To Kill A Mockingbird*. I read all the Peanuts Gang collections, and every Time Life book on World War II. Today, my favorites are Hemingway, Carver, O'Connor, Fitzgerald, Moore, Rash, and Talese. Gatsby is much better at 40 than 14. I acquired a taste for poetry after discovering Collins, Makuck, Chappell, Heaney, Hayden and McKean.

Because we were so far out in the country, many miles from the nearest library, an old converted school bus known as the bookmobile made the rounds in our end of the county, with a regular stop at a country store a few miles down the road. This library-on-wheels was a treat to look forward to all summer. I still remember the smell that enveloped me as soon as the hiss of the doors sounded and I climbed aboard. We didn't have central air conditioning in our house, and the bookmobile had a friendly chill to it, the cold air offering a break from the stifling summer heat. It was the smell of aging paper and glue and binding and book jackets and the hands and homes that had touched the books. It was being in the presence of words stacked floor to ceiling, higher than I could reach, that transported me to another place even though we never left the yard.

Since Mama and I were the only patrons, the library eventually made our house an official bookmobile stop, and the two ladies who drove it would load us down new editions every two weeks. They seemed as excited to have readers as we did to have things to read.

As I got older, most of my friends started reading *Sports Illustrated*, but I preferred *The Sporting News* — it was still published on newsprint, and the writing from the venerable reporters and columnists such as Art Spander, Furman Bisher, Peter Gammons, Peter Vecsey and Dick Young had much so more style and depth. I loved stories that put me in places and ballparks and cities I dreamed of seeing one day, stories that could make me see and touch and smell the surroundings — stories that I wanted to write.

• • •

Writing is no different than sports or photography. Talent comes in handy, but really, it is sweat that makes it work. That, not talent, is how I made a living behind the camera for so long.

Those who have known me a long time must think I'm having one hell of a midlife crisis, going to school, writing and teaching college

English. I love it because the more I teach writing, the more I learn about it. Writers outgrow stories, much like clothes, as the writer gets taller and broader and the work adds maturity.

It has taken me a long time to realize a career can be enjoyed, but in the end it is just a job. A calling is a passion that may burn at different temperatures, but never flickers out.

• • •

4

Small Game

"There he is!" shouted my brother.

I had my shotgun pointed down at the ground, but quickly swung it up to my shoulder. I flicked the safety off with the thumb of my right hand, lined up my shot, and pulled the trigger.

As the firing pin struck the primer, there was a flash, explosion and kick. The power of a .410 shotgun, while considered a small gauge, is still impressive. My ears numbed as the shot echoed off the edge of the woods on the far western point of the farm, and the pungent but pleasing aroma of gunpowder blew back in my face. I could feel my heartbeat throbbing in my cheeks and ears, but there was complete silence, save my instinctive "click-clack" ejecting of the green shell casing and the sliding of the safety back on.

It had all happened in two seconds, maybe less. I waited for the smoke to clear to see what I had done.

• • •

I got my first gun for Christmas when I was 13 years old. I'll never forget waking up that morning and finding the long, narrow, plain cardboard box that held my brand new Remington. It was a complete surprise. I had been asking for a gun every Christmas for as long as I could remember, so I could hunt and shoot skeet and generally be manly enough to hang out more with my brother, Bill, who was 10 years older, and possibly the coolest guy I knew.

The gun was a work of art, the metal bluing smooth and flawless, and the brand and specs stamped on top near the breach. The wood finish was dark walnut, with lots of visible grain, just like my dad's rifles and shotguns that he kept locked in his bedroom. Most importantly, my shotgun was pump action, just like my dad's favorite 12-gauge, the one my brother and I would always argue over when it was time to hunt or target shoot. Daddy's Sears Ted Williams model semiautomatic was smoother and faster and more accurate, but there was something about a pump action — the racking, the fluidity acquired through practice, and the timing required to realign that made that gun more appealing to shoot.

For the rest of that Christmas break, tin cans, pie pans, clay targets all became casualties of my obsession with practice and accuracy. I had seen Daddy's medals for marksmanship in Korea, and wondered if that was a trait that could be passed on. I didn't want to leave it to chance, so I practiced. Santa had provided ammo, but two boxes didn't last long. I don't think Mama particularly cared for the constant gunfire going on in the backyard. I don't know how she controlled the protective urges over her baby, the youngest of five children by a good measure.

• • •

When I was around nine, I was allowed to use Bill's old lever action Daisy alone in the yard. Even though the gun could not propel a BB fast enough to break a tin pie pan at 20 feet, I was certain I would be able to keep crows out of the corn, take down some birds for supper and possibly kill a bear, despite the fact I'd never seen one on the farm. Daddy and Bill had drilled gun safety into me from what seemed like the crib: Every gun is loaded. Never take a gun more powerful than a BB gun out of the rack without an adult present. Always carry a gun with the barrel pointed at the ground. It is acceptable to carry a gun on your shoulder, but not if there is anyone behind you. When climbing a fence or crossing a stream, lay the gun down where you are going, barrel pointed away, first. Anywhere you can't do this, don't go. Never look in a barrel. Never swing a gun parallel. Safeties might be off even when they look on. Empty a firearm before entering a house, load outside. Never clean a gun with anyone else in the room. Never shoot without knowing what is behind what you're shooting at. Never hunt anything you don't plan to eat, with the exceptions of rodents and pests.

These principles were not exclusive to my family. Guns are an essential component of the home in rural North Carolina. They help put food on the table and provide home protection where the nearest law enforcement is often a half hour away. In high school, many classmates went hunting before class during deer and duck season, and hung their shotguns and rifles in gun racks in the back windows of locked pickup trucks. The FFA chapter had a skeet shooting team, and they practiced on school grounds, just like the athletic teams.

• • •

That Thanksgiving of my last squirrel hunt with Bill was one where the sky looked like it does an hour after sunset, all day long. Bill lived with his wife and newborn on the north side of the farm. He came by early for a pre-lunch trek to the woods.

Despite the warmth of my bed, and a rare day to sleep in, I was up quickly. I pulled on old jeans, a flannel shirt, and my hunting vest that had slots for plenty of rounds. It was ironic that in a dozen forays into the woods over the previous two seasons, I had fired a total of one time at a squirrel, but had room on my vest for an entire box of shells.

I grabbed a biscuit as we headed out the door, and felt the pinpricks of cold on my face that foretold winter. We hiked just past the soybean field that in less than a decade would become the lot on which my wife and I would move a mobile home, and then later build a house. But that day, the field ended at a two-track path the width of a tractor. We found an opening in the poplar, pines, oaks, black walnuts and maples, and started our walk, careful not to drag feet across dry leaves. We looked for evidence of our prey: cracked acorns, nutshells or scat. We had never hunted there before.

Some hunters stalk squirrels or use dogs. Bill's method was to find a quiet place with a good field of vision, a spot where the hunter could sit on the ground with his back against a tree. He would drop me off and then move farther along for his own spot, where we'd have safe ranges of fire. Then we sat and waited.

A hunted grey squirrel can sit perfectly still and not make a sound for at least an hour. These animals are not the type you find in parks and on college campuses, a pet-like fur ball that will approach a human out of curiosity and desire for a handout. Grey squirrels in the wild are crafty, smart survivors. They are athletic. You rarely see fat squirrels, because fat squirrels are slow, and slow squirrels don't live long among foxes, coyotes, owls, hawks and other predators.

Unlike my brother, I was not a natural outdoorsman. Never growing out of childhood impatience or desire for action, I had long ago given up on pond fishing. I just couldn't handle the sitting and waiting and swatting insects in the heat of summer, nor did I have any desire to dine on catfish, crappie or bream. But hunting was different. Deep in the woods, trying to be still, required concentration and heightened the senses. Once the hunt began, Bill and I didn't talk until we exited the woods. I sat and listened and thought. I heard leaves rustling, and then nothing. I wondered about the hunters who came before us, how much of the landscape was the same. Some trees were bigger and some had fallen, but essentially the forest floor was unchanged in the last 100 years or so. I thought about local history, how soldiers had camped in woods just like these, for shelter and protection from hunters in blue or gray or red, and I considered the haunts of a sentry's imagination when hearing the same rustling I heard. My brother and I were the only armed people in those woods. What sheer terror it must have been to hear footsteps, to be the prey, not the predator, and to know the only defense was a primitive, one-shot musket. I thought about what my future would be like, what I would do, how I would one day return to the same woods with my son and show him the same places I once sat.

Time slipped away quickly that morning. After a couple of hours, Bill walked over to me.

"Seen anything?" he asked.

"Nothing. How about you?"

"Not a thing. Let's go eat."

We went back through the opening and had just stepped on the path when my brother shouted. I realize now he passed on the shot for me to take it. I didn't hesitate and tracked the squirrel across my sights as he jumped from one branch to the other. He seemed as big as a dog. I fired. Before the smoke, I saw him flip downward.

"You got 'im!" Bill shouted.

We hustled over to the edge of the woods, not wanting to let a wounded animal get away and suffer. That was another rule. "He's a nice one." Bill said. "Good shot."

I didn't know how the squirrel would taste, but I knew it couldn't be better than that sounded.

• • •

Even in the hands of a skilled knifeman, dressing game is at once violent, graphic, bloody and real. Back at the house, my brother pulled out his hunting knife, and dispatched the head, paws and tail of the squirrel. I presumed he learned this from Daddy. He handed me the tail as a souvenir from the first kill, saying we'd preserve it (which we didn't) and then proceeded to peel the hide off the squirrel like a doll's jacket. The squirrel seemed much smaller in this state, and it was obvious that it would take a bagful of them to feed a family. He washed the carcass under an outdoor spigot and used the knife to remove the spent pellets. I fetched a zipper bag from the kitchen and he tossed the meat into Mama's freezer with assurances that we would cook and eat it soon. We never did.

That was the last time I went squirrel hunting. While I thought my brother and I would hunt together forever, that was one of our last outings in search of small game. We went dove hunting the next two seasons, which was far more challenging and rewarding, and we grilled our success the night of the hunts. But by that point, I had come to realize that hunting was not going to be a long-term interest. The image of that field dressed squirrel has never left me. There is an old saw in sports that says you have to be able to see yourself making the shot, or the catch, first, before you can complete it. I never could see myself pursuing, killing and cleaning. That was what I took away that morning, rather than food for the table.

I preferred competition, whether it be skeet, or handguns, or rifles. This was part of the appeal later when I earned my concealed carry permit — a certain number of shots had to be placed in a specific range in a fixed amount of time to qualify (in addition to safety training, a written test and a background check). Sport.

The following falls, I hunted pickup basketball games, choosing well-placed elbows and turnaround baseline jumpers to do my dirty work, rather than a long, sharp, unsheathed blade.

• • •

My boys, eight and six now, frequently ask about fishing and hunting. My wife, whose grandparents lived on the Neuse River, usually takes them fishing. I have suggested we might try fly fishing, something I've never done, because it is active, and they were intrigued by "A River Runs Through It." Hunting is yet to come.

My eight year old asks when I will allow him to have a BB gun. He and his brother are avid readers of *Outdoor Life* and *Saltwater Fisherman*. We've already talked about gun safety quite a bit, and I've made no secret about where the guns are kept — locked — and how they are to be feared, respected and handled. The boys' time will come soon enough, and I won't deny them the experience. I want to share it with them, much like we do sports now. I appreciate those moments, because Daddy never played basketball or catch or went hunting with me, and I have kept that promise to myself that Kent and Lowell will never have such a void. We'll go in those same woods one day, and find our spot and wait. I don't know if the boys, who are more energetic than I was, will appreciate the quiet time and the concentration required. But I hope they don't kill anything. I never learned how to field dress a squirrel.

• • •

5

The Handler

I opened the door to the gray-and-wood paneled Mercury, climbed into the worn, burgundy-cloth front seat and didn't say a word. I didn't look up from my green Sears Toughskin jeans, the kind with the double reinforced knee patches, and wiped a tear or two on my homemade shirt. I didn't look at Mama, but I could feel the heat on my left cheek.

"What's wrong?" Mama asked.

Silence.

"You might as well tell me, because I'm going to find out," she said. "Did you get in trouble or did something happen? I'm going to sit here 'til you tell me."

Despite the line of cars stretched out behind her, I knew she wasn't kidding.

The only things I got in trouble for were being bored and daydreaming, or talking too much, and Mama knew that was only good for a note on my report card, maybe a "Needs Improvement" under conduct, but nothing to cry over. So I told her. My fourth grade teacher had accused me of plagiarism on a history report. Mama was all about education. She was determined that the best way off the farm for the child who had no inclination for row crops or livestock, but instead preferred a desk and a lamp and history books, was college. Elementary school was none-too-soon to be thinking about this. Her face flushed, and she white-knuckled that old station wagon out of the half-circle drive, onto the street and back into the school parking lot.

In a flash, all 5-foot-4 inches, 100 pounds of her was out of the car, telling me to stay put. She stopped long enough to say something to the teacher on duty and point at me before she disappeared into the building.

I was sure my life was over. Mrs. Finch was trouble enough without Mama making it worse; Finch was notorious for demeaning and embarrassing students for such offenses as laughing in class, or some other perceived failure of decorum. She firmly believed in keeping order through humiliation. But now my teacher was going to have to deal with The Handler.

• • •

Mama is now a grandmother 14 times over (not counting the great-grandchildren), known as the sweet little lady who has taught the Wide Awakes Sunday Class at Momeyer Baptist Church for over 50 years. She has such a dry sense of humor, most of her comments and jokes breeze right by people.

She was raised on a tobacco farm during the Depression. Most of her clothes were made out of feed bags, which processors wove in patterns, knowing their clients who owned chickens were recycling the material into dresses and shirts. A big Christmas meant an orange in her stocking, and maybe some penny candy. Mama and her sisters and brother knew hard times.

Consolidation sent her and her classmates from the small country schoolhouse to a nearby town for high school. There was definitely friction between the social classes — "town" versus "country." This is where Mama learned to stand her ground.

This is also where Mama turned inward and became more clannish.

Her closest friends were kinfolk, those who were understanding, shared the same Christian values and could be counted on. While newcomers are greeted warmly in our ever-expanding tribe, they still have to walk an unseen line, to provide proof of a good heart and loyalty. Regular visits are expected, as well as regular attendance at functions and holidays. Family is at the center of everything for Mama, what the world revolves around, the only thing that matters.

• • •

It seemed like Mama was inside the school forever. All the kids in the car line had been picked up, I'd grown tired of reading my library book, and still there was no sign of her.

My tears had long since dried up. I was ready to go home, to forget this whole thing. I could not imagine a scene or an outcome where I would be able to survive Mrs. Finch's class for several more months — my God, it wasn't even Christmas yet. I was sure to feel blowback.

I checked my Mickey Mouse watch. I was usually home by now, well into reading the Raleigh *News and Observer* and enjoying an ice cold Orange Crush in a glass bottle, the afternoon delight of my elementary school life. Finally, about the time I started putting serious thought into what branch of the military I'd have to join because Mama had been gone too long for any good to come about, she materialized from the double doors at the bottom of the staircase. She didn't look happy, but there was a calm resolution about her. The Marines would have to wait; maybe everything would be okay after all.

• • •

When I was about nine or ten years old, my bookkeeper uncle mentioned to Mama that one of his clients was looking for a dessert supplier for his lunch counter in Rocky Mount. His restaurant had a line out the door during the tobacco market season, known as a place you could get a great homemade hamburger or hot dog. Customers then clamored for something to satisfy a sweet tooth. Mama had a reputation for cakes and pies of all sorts, so my uncle asked if she wanted to take a few of those coconut crème, coconut custard, and chocolate meringue pies, wrap them individually, and see if they sold.

Mama had been using her culinary skills for all sorts of bribery and palm greasing over the years. We had an old-school family doctor who had his practice at a crossroads in an adjoining county, across the road from the seed store on one side and a 76 gas station on the other. Dr. Stallings was a gracious man of modest demeanor. He took patients on a first-come, first-served basis, beginning at 7:30 a.m. and ending when the last patient had been seen, Monday through Saturday. It was well-known that the good doctor, whose client base fell mostly under the poverty line, often would take chickens and hams and other forms of payment from those who needed medical attention but had no cash. Mama worked the system this way: she would check in with the one of the gatekeepers, a nurse or sometimes, the doctor's wife, and while we always paid cash, Mama would slip a still-warm cake or pie across the counter. At a time when it was rumored folks might sit all day waiting to be seen, we never sat in the car more than two hours. Mama refused to sit in the waiting room with "the sick folks," because they usually looked worse than we did, she said.

• • •

Boy, did those sweets sell at the grill. What started as a once a week drop off soon became an almost everyday delivery run. Other restaurants called. Margie's Bake Shop was born.

I never thought about it then, but when I look back now, I don't know how she did it. Three of her five children still lived at home, and she kept us all clothed and fed. I never ate a store-bought vegetable until I moved out for college, as our farm produced a year's worth of canning and freezing. When we had cows and pigs, we put up our own meat, as well. She cleaned the house, did the laundry, got us to school, and even worked part time for a while at the local high school cafeteria. Although Daddy worked the farm and a day job, it apparently was not enough. Instead of complaining though, Mama just got it done.

Pretty soon, she added other grills, some local grocery stores and a large chain store. Later, when I got my driver's license, I made deliveries and during the holidays, when I was home from college on break, I'd stay up until 3 a.m. to bake the bestselling item, a soft, yeast sourdough roll. Mama literally could not make enough to fill demand in November and December.

It was only recently that I realized that the piece of paper hanging on my office wall from Barton College is not made from parchment, but rather cocoa, custard and light, fluffy dough.

•　•　•

Mama got in and shut the car door and cranked the engine.

"What have you done?" I asked. "I'm dead."

"Oh no you're not. You know, I don't mean this ugly, but who can't tell the difference in something a fourth-grader writes and something out of a book? That woman's got a real problem."

"How bad was it?" I asked. "Do I have to go to school somewhere else?"

"Don't be silly. I told her that you were not a cheater, 'cause if you were, I would have taken care of that before that durn paper had ever been turned in. I still can't get over her accusing you of *cheating*."

I said nothing. I was comforted by Mama's confidence, but I wasn't so sure there would be smooth sailing. Mrs. Finch did not seem to be the forgive-and-forget type.

"But that's not even what really made me mad."

Oh, God. There had to be a "but."

"After we, um, settled the paper thing, she told me that you ask a lot of stupid questions. She also said you stand up a lot when she is writing

46

stuff on the board and she has to tell you to sit down everyday. She said you're a real pain in the neck."

I carefully measured how to respond. I'd never considered a teacher might feel that way about me.

"So then I asked her to show me where you sit. She said that since you are so tall, she makes you sit in the back. She said it real smart alecky, too. I didn't think too much of that." There was a pause. "Can you not see the board?"

I could not.

Mama went on, "I'm calling the eye doctor when we get home. Then I might be the one asking Mrs. Finch some stupid questions, like, how did you get to be a teacher?"

I've always felt Mama left out a lot of details. Mrs. Finch had very little to say to me the rest of the school year.

• • •

Mama was alone not long after she and Daddy married, as he was drafted and sent to Korea, his first trip out of the state. While he was gone, my oldest brother was born, and Mama lived the life of a single parent at 19.

When Daddy got home, he farmed and worked other jobs, first for a defense contractor, then a wood products company, and later for a welding supply business. I don't know exactly what Daddy did and saw in Korea, because he has always given short answers about his service that amount to no answers. His records show Signal Corps, but he also has an Expert Marksman medal and a few rows of ribbons. As a boy, I saw him knock down crows in our cornfield with a .22 rifle, one right behind the other, which he then had me string up as a warning to other crows. "They're smart," he said. "They'll get the idea."

Mama said his nightmares went on for years, and that he was never the happy, easygoing teenager she fell in love with. I only knew the sad, often frustrated, short tempered, quickly remorseful man. Before they even had a name for it, Daddy had Post Traumatic Stress Disorder, or

PTSD. It would take decades for the Army to recognize this, and Mama took up the fight for years, especially when it became difficult for Daddy, towards the end of his working career, to stay focused and even-keeled. He had managed to push down the mood swings until the early 1990s when he had open-heart surgery. Gruff and sharp-tongued, he was overcome in the days before the night before. The man thought he was going to die, and I wasn't so sure he wasn't right.

Mama has never left his side, even when you could see the toll taken on her. It has continued in the 20 years since, as Daddy has not proven to be a good patient, growling at Mama, his caretaker, sometimes refusing medication, and most often being hard to get along with. She makes all of his appointments, tracks prescriptions and coordinates all the trips to various VA locations. She then becomes his navigator and advocate, speaking softly most of the time and carrying a nice, big loaf of sourdough when the situation arises. Those frozen Korean nights left Daddy with nearly incapacitating arthritis at times, and the side effects of the treatments were often as bad as the pain. Mama continued to jump through hoops at the Veteran's Administration, an agency that counts on most claimants to give up or die before benefits are ever approved. But Mama was like a pit bull, shuffling through mountains of paperwork from doctors substantiating conditions and causes. Mama said that Daddy sat quietly through most of the interviews, distracted or disinterested, and said as little as possible. A little research into PTSD evidences this as shame or embarrassment from being unable to control a situation; add into this that Daddy came from a generation where assistance or any type of mental health care was scorned, and depression becomes inevitable.

Finally, one day when Mama was about ready to give up, she took him for a meeting with his VA rep. Breaking routine, she dropped him at the door and went to park the car. That unguarded moment would prove pivotal. When she got inside, she could hear a loud, profanity-laced tirade in the familiar voice. She scolded Daddy like a child, calmed him down and returned to the rep to apologize. He told her it was the best thing that could have happened, and that it was long overdue. A report of the episode was enough to clear the last hurdle after a decade-long battle. Handlers always step in to control a situation, they are fixers, but sometimes that backfires, sometimes running interference can have a negative effect.

• • •

There is a flat, woven basket on the counter at my parents' house. This is where all the medications are kept. I never remember Mama taking much medicine when I was a kid, and even now as she glides toward 80, she really only takes a pill to hold off glaucoma. A lifelong reader, like her mother, her worst, quietly-held fear is the thought of not being able to ease into the corner of the couch with her Bible or a good volume of nonfiction. Daddy takes quite a few now, ranging from those for pain to "calmers" for PTSD to injections for Type II diabetes, which he somehow managed to dodge until his seventies. Mama administers them all. It is not easy. Despite her denials, she has been known to resort to methods right out of "Arsenic and Old Lace."

My nephew Chris loves to tell the story about the day he stopped in just as Mama was putting breakfast on the table. He reached over to help himself to some eggs and Mama stopped him.

"You don't want those," she said.

"They look good to me."

"Trust me. I'll fix you some more. But those are special eggs. For your granddaddy."

Thus began the legend of Mama breaking up meds into some dishes, and the running joke of whether a particular dish is "special" during family dinners. She is not amused at the jokes we make. But, she deserves the peace. Daddy can be difficult on his best days, and her most stressful time is the daily insulin injections. He often resorts to conduct similar to that of my grade school boys — he resists the shots, overreacts, demands foods he's not supposed to eat and competes for attention.

The family functions are what get Mama through the tough days.

Sundays after church have always been a traditional time for lunch at her house. For years, she put on a spread that would rival any restaurant buffet — a table set with barbecued chicken, or homemade pot pie or meatloaf or carved ham, plenty of country vegetables, sourdough bread and at least two desserts. As the family has aged, and some have moved on to other traditions or other parts of the country, the Sunday meal has been scaled back, and it is now more of a covered dish affair. Mama still monitors plates and conversations, and most often becomes the sounding board for any and all troubles. This extends past Sundays, and through the week, and Mama is always ready to step into the breach, to do whatever is needed, to make sure what needs to be done, is.

There were plenty of absolutes for us children, even though I belong to a different generation than my siblings. We were always in church on Sunday mornings. No one went to bed until homework was not only done, it was done correctly. Everyone had chores. Christmas was a big deal. So were birthdays.

There were things that even Mama couldn't control. In the course of less than eight years, she lost a son-in-law, her sister/best friend and her mother, and she still grieves for each of them everyday, especially at night when she used to talk on the phone just before bedtime to my aunt and grandmother. As the family has grown exponentially, there are from time to time some minor and temporarily major fractures, and these things, too, have taken a toll. Things now tend to hurt her feelings more than bring out her fighting side. People unload their burdens and ask for favors. She has always amazed me with her energy, and when she retired from the bakery business, she came to work for me at my photography studio when my wife went out on maternity leave. She ran circles around me, climbing ladders, scooting under tables, listening to clients' troubles and never sitting still.

But now, especially after she has chased behind my children, the youngest three of her grandchildren, she finally, sometimes, seems tired. To them, there is nothing their Mammy can't do. They know that all they have to do is ask, and Mama will handle it.

• • •

The worst thing and the best thing about that episode in fourth grade was that I got glasses. I later overhead the optometrist tell Mama that my vision without them was 20/400. The entire world came into a nice, sharp focus for the first time, and of course, the barbs of "four eyes" and "spaz" and "nerd" soon followed. It was a good trade, though, and I knew for sure that no matter what, Mama had my back.

• • •

6

Warm Sunday Nights

A friend stopped by my studio to talk to me about making a photograph of an old house for her so she could get it insured for her employer. We talked for a bit, and she mentioned that if I was still interested in getting rid of the old fuel oil drum behind my building, her husband would like to get it. I was more than happy to see it go; the removal would give me a valuable extra parking space in the tight back alley of Nashville's downtown array of century-old buildings.

"If he wants this heater," I said, motioning to the old Siegler in the middle of the open floor, "he is welcome to it. Maybe for his workshop. All I want out of it is someone to cap the stovepipe opening in the ceiling."

Our business concluded, my friend showed herself out the backdoor, hesitating just long enough to allow a raw November draft to slice through the back hallway, making me shiver. I put my hands in my pants pockets, stepped over in front of the Siegler and shifted from one foot to the other, the way folks move when they are trying to shake off a chill.

The only problem was that the unit wasn't turned on. It was out of fuel, much like the business and the owner with whom it shared a building.

. . .

On Sunday nights in the cold gray of winter, Mama would make me pimento cheese sandwiches, toasted in the oven in a pie pan. There would always be a warm bowl of Campbell's tomato soup to go with it. Maybe it was the way the bread crusted just a bit, and the cheese softened inside it, paired just right with the simple tanginess of the soup, that made it the perfect comfort food. No toaster or modern oven can mimic the results of Mama's old worn out GE. Unlike all the other meals of the week, when the whole family would sit and eat together at the kitchen table, Mama would let me sit on the floor in front of our Siegler heater in the living room and watch television or read the Sunday newspaper. It was sports, then entertainment and arts — I always saved the comics for last. My favorite show on those nights was "The Southern Sportsman," a locally produced hunting and fishing show. Each week, the host, Frank White, showed grainy home movie-quality film of hunting or fishing expeditions, and ended each show with the catchphrase, "Do yourself a favor, take a kid fishing." I neither hunted nor fished regularly, but was hooked on the idea of this show.

On school mornings, that spot in front of the heater was my layover from the bed to the breakfast table. Like our soot-black pug, I'd curl up and let the warm air blow across my back; sometimes I'd have to force her out of my spot, which she yielded with grunts and sighs before circling around and snugging up to next to me. A boy's life was good at times.

. . .

The old farmhouse I grew up in had its share of drafts. The original structure dated back to the early part of the 20th century. It was plated in an odd and short-lived fad known as "German shingles" — a fragile, ugly, and impractical ceramic siding. Our shingles were old and beige and brittle, and I cracked more than one with errant fastballs. At some point, a mobile home was added as an extension to the front of the house, creating an extra two bedrooms as well as a mini-kitchen for our family of seven, of which I was the "baby" by a good ten years. The house was cooled with a couple of window unit air conditioners, and heated exclusively with the Siegler.

Siegler made a reliable heater before ceasing production in the 1950s. Constructed of thin metal, the most popular units were slightly smaller than an average refrigerator, seemed twice as heavy, and came in a two-tone brown-on-beige color scheme. Midway up the unit was a window with a metal latch that opened to a steel door with a smaller window that contained the cast-iron boiler. At the bottom of a heater was a vent, about the size of most residential floor vents today. Blower controls were on the back or right side, with temperature settings of Hi, Lo and Med. Lighting the thing seemed like a hazard in itself, as fuel oil had to bleed into the burner — not too little, not too much — before a wooden kitchen match was struck and tossed into the bottom. A roar and a fireball signaled success.

Eastern North Carolina is not a place that immediately comes to mind as a wintry region. But it is certainly a myth that the temperature is mild year round. We had sleet, snow, ice and wind. The Siegler was a gathering place in those days for my family: some sitting in chairs, some standing and rubbing hands together, just in from a farm chore, and me usually on the floor. One of my brothers might tell about helping the neighbor chase his cows back into the pasture; Daddy would talk about what part of the old Farmall needed fixing; and Mama would plan supper, deciding what she needed me to fetch from the smokehouse or freezer.

Modern forced air systems are most certainly safer, more economical, and efficient and provide better distribution, but I'd dispute that they are better. Now that I have three young children, it is hard not to think about how much better time could be spent gathered around an old metal box heater, talking and reading and warming. Climate controlled evenings with electronic devices doesn't seem like something children will have warm memories of someday. No one sits around a floor vent and talks about basketball, the farm report, or what would be good for Sunday dinner.

• • •

I jumped at the chance to move my studio up to Washington Street, on the main thoroughfare in the county seat. The building sits across the street from the Courthouse, which was built in 1921. Some folks refer to my place as "The 1913 Building," that date of its construction laid out in brickwork on the façade. It was originally built as a dry goods store, spent time as a clothing store and prior to my purchase, had been a well-known antique shop for three decades. Two of the original glass top counters remain, as do the original stock shelves that line the space for almost 40 feet on either side. The floors are ancient hardwood, protected for a century under various layers of oriental rugs and other carpets, creak rhythmically with every step. The building is just one of two left in town with an intricate tin ceiling. The newest technological advance visible is the 1960s fluorescent lights, and if not for the digital cameras and my Mac computers, an out-of-town visitor might have thought he'd stumbled into an exhibit change at the local museum.

There is a basement, where you can still see the old double doors — bricked in now — that offered a place to park the horse carriage or Model T in the early days. A few steps up from the sales floor is a mezzanine with an old style railing and a frosted glass accounting office that looks straight out of the set of the "Maltese Falcon" or "The Big Sleep." It is not hard to imagine a stern, visor-wearing manager or owlish bookkeeper watching over the salespeople below, making sure the store got its money's worth in labor.

It takes a lot of fuel oil to heat 2,400 feet of office space with 20-foot high ceilings, and no insulation. I ordered a thermal heater from an online company and made do with that. Part of me wants to fire up that old heater, and see what it will do. I used the excuse that the relic was too expensive to operate, but maybe deep down I was worried I'd spend too much time sitting in front of it.

• • •

My grandma, my Mama's mama, had a heater identical to ours. Unlike Mama, Granny didn't like for me to sit so close to the heater. She always fretted about me getting burned, or it not being good for me, or some other potential hazard. Granny was a worrier, even more than Mama. She knew a life where having shoes year round was a luxury, flu epidemics ravaged the country, and the Great Depression stole a huge chunk of her youth. My granddaddy, who died of a stroke before I was born, left Granny to be a widow for half a century. She had her Bible, a TV for Billy Graham Crusades, the church nearby, a farm to rent out and the Siegler for heat.

There is not a single time I can remember visiting my grandmother from November through March when she didn't have the old Siegler heater roiling and something sweet baking in her kitchen.

• • •

Mama and Daddy got rid of their old heater in the early 1980s when they remodeled the house. Along with a central heating and air system, they installed a wood stove. Daddy's enthusiasm for stockpiling firewood often made me wonder if the man intended to clear-cut the entire state before Reagan's first term was up. The wood heater was nice, but it wasn't long into that first winter before Daddy called the salesman back to hook a blower fan to the heater — we all agreed that something was missing. Whether we wanted to admit it or not, we missed the old Siegler.

The wood stove lasted through my undergrad years, and the smell and feel of wood heat has a comfort of its own. That era would not last though, as the in-house labor force (me) was preparing to leave the nest. My folks finally transitioned to gas logs. Blowers are available for those things as well. Despite the store displays, gas logs aren't all that quaint. Mama and Daddy seldom fire them up now, mostly relying on the thermostat to regulate a consistent temperature. No one eats pimento cheese sandwiches and tomato soup in front of a thermostat.

• • •

My friend's now ex-husband hasn't been to get the oil drum or the old heater yet, and I'm not sure he will. I asked around for months to see if any of my friends knew of anyone who might be cold over the winter and could use a good, dependable, free heater. While nostalgic, it is still quite practical and would serve a cold soul well.

What I'm not sure of is how I'm going to feel when the heater is gone. It is not the Siegler that sat in my parents' living room. Even so, it was fueled not just by the oil put into it, but the stories told around it, just like ours. Its new owners will take heat from it, and add another layer to the memories stored in the Siegler. It will be warm.

• • •

7

Tea Cookies

Granny — my mother's mother — made things unlikely to be found in stores: caramel cake, coconut meringue pie, sea foam candy and chocolate "candy" icing. But nothing came close to her tea cookies.

Tea cookies were a simple concoction. They weren't anything like what TV food celebrities crow about in overdone Southern accents as they make what amounts to mini-biscuits. Flour, sugar, baking powder, baking soda, eggs, buttermilk, butter, a pinch of salt and a little vanilla extract went into the bowl — never measured, just eyeballed. Granny would beat up the dough, throw it out on a flour-dusted cloth and run her roller back and forth until the batter looked as though it might disappear. I wondered how much of that thinness was out of a lifelong habit of stretching ingredients, and how much actually mattered to the construction of the cookie. The dough was cut into circles with a vegetable chopper, and placed on a baking pan.

It would seem that putting such thin pieces of dough into an oven would result in either a burned, brittle shingle or a cookie so hard it would be inedible. Granny knew just how long was long enough. She yanked the pan out of the oven, and scooped the cookies onto a cloth baking sheet, admonishing my cousins and I not to touch the treats until they had cooled, or we would get horribly disfiguring burn wounds. No doubt that anticipation made the tea cookies sweeter, and just one opening of the oven door would envelope the whole house in a fog of "freshly baked." I've only seen one written copy of the recipe, Scotch-taped to the inside of a cabinet in Mama's kitchen; she is the only person in the entire family who knows how to make the cookies. She hardly ever makes them, even though they rival Granny's finest. Mama says hers just aren't as good.

My cousins all preferred their cookies to be lathered in chocolate candy icing that Granny would make in small batches on the stove, using condensed milk, Hershey's cocoa, powdered sugar, and butter.

Granny was still cranking those tea cookies out well into her 80s, and they only got better every year. It was art.

I preferred my cookies plain. They were perfect as far as I was concerned — crispy, sweet and buttery — and it seemed wrong to mess with that. I always thought they were the best things anyone could ever eat, and nothing was as warm as getting the kitchen chair closest to the living room heater and digging into a plate of warm tea cookies.

• • •

8

The Indian Hole

Someone walked lightly through the kitchen. With the covers pulled up to my nose, and my eyes wide open, I sat as still as possible and listened to find out if I really heard it.

Then I heard it again, the tension of an adult stepping on old wood, and the light above the kitchen sink cast a shadow on the open door to my bedroom. I expected to hear Mama or Daddy open the refrigerator for something to drink. They didn't. The creak continued, but got quieter, then stopped. Then silence. It was always worst in the middle of the summer, but the next year, when my folks got the first window unit air conditioner for my room, I didn't hear the sounds as much.

I pulled the covers up higher, rolled over, and tried to go to sleep. I was eight. Mama told me on other nights when this happened that I was just hearing things. I had my doubts.

• • •

The sisters knew the only relief from the record-setting, 100-degree July heat that was crushing eastern North Carolina was to head for the cool waters of the Tar River, just a mile's walk away, across two tobacco farms. Never mind air conditioning; in the midst of the Depression, there was no electricity in any of the homes on the dusty dirt road where the girls lived.

With their chores done, the Winstead sisters — Mamie Harriet, 21; Mary Frances, 18; and their baby sister, Eula Pearl, 9 — set off across the field to see if their friend, Effie Brantley, wanted to go wading, and more importantly to see if her daddy, Mr. Burt would chaperone.

Mr. Burt met the girls in the yard and told them his daughter was sick and she would not be going to the river. He also offered them a warning.

"Y'all don't need to be going down to that river by yourselves," he told them.

"Mr. Burt, I'm plenty grown to go," Mamie Harriet said.

"I know you've growed up, but y'all don't know where that Indian Hole is," he said. "By the time you get in it, you can't get out. It can take the lot of you straight to the bottom of that river. Me and your daddy knows where it is. Y'all don't. Lot of folks been caught in that thing and never come back."

"Mr. Burt, you and Daddy always tell that story, but I ain't never heard of nobody drowning down there. Besides, we just want to wade and cool off," said Mary Frances. "It's so hot."

"Y'all don't need to go and I ain't going to leave Effie. And you know your daddy would have a fit if y'all went without somebody to look after you."

"Alright, Mr. Burt. We're just going to go up and see what Lottie is doing then," said Mamie Harriet.

"Alright then," Mr. Burt said. "But y'all stay out of that river."

The sisters headed down the path toward the Strickland farm. They were willowy, slender from hard labor, all three with pigtails and dresses made from seed bags — seed companies had started using designs on their sacks because they knew farm folks were fashioning clothes from them out of necessity. The sun beat down on their brown hair, which had lightened to near blonde from a summer spent outside working the farm with their daddy and brothers.

At the Strickland house, Lottie, 16, was swinging from a rope tied to a branch in an old Magnolia tree. Another friend, Juanita Lewis, was sitting on the ground, propped against the tree.

Dozens of deaths caused by the unrelenting heat wave were reported in newspapers across the country every day that summer. There was no relief to be had on the farm, and the temptation of the water pulled hard at the girls. It didn't take much to convince Lottie and Juanita to cut across the Strickland's back field and down to the banks of the Tar. The river was only about 30 yards wide at that point, and they decided they'd just walk out to where it was waist deep. None of them could swim.

Eula Pearl was the first in, squealing and pulling her sisters and their friends into the murky, green water. Somebody said watch out for snakes. They all held hands. The water felt so good as it ran over their dusty clothes, rushing over ankles and thighs and hips. So cool. The older girls dipped their faces into the water, untied pigtails and leaned their heads back. The old river was aptly named, dark and ugly as it cut a path across a third of the state, but it didn't matter on that day as the water felt icy cold on its meander towards the Atlantic.

Eula Pearl watched a dragonfly skim the surface, mesmerized by its almost drunken flight path, not even realizing she'd stepped into a crevice that brought the water to her chest. And then, Eula Pearl felt a tug at her feet. She stumbled, and felt a hard pull. Unsure whether something had grabbed her, Eula Pearl held tightly onto Mamie Harriet's arm and yelled out. It seemed like someone was under the water —a savage, maybe — grasping at legs. In a blink, Mamie Harriet felt the same pull, and the other three girls realized this was not a game or a joke. Mary Frances dug her heels into the sludgy, silty bottom, trying to dig in and pull her sisters back to safety while her friends tugged at her arms and waist.

In the space of seconds, Pearl disappeared beneath the green-black surface and Mamie Harriet was flailing up and down, struggling to stand up and gasp for air. The girls shrieked and yelled but no one was close enough to hear them. It wouldn't have mattered. Mamie Harriet went under and didn't come back up. Lottie and Juanita had retreated several feet from their positions, and Mary Frances was now feeling the pull and yelling for her sisters. Panicked, she held onto her friends with her other hand. Lottie and Juanita could feel the coils of something strange moving across the tops of their feet, not a solid or real thing, but not just river water. Just as Mary Frances was yanked below the surface, they slipped and stumbled backwards as if they'd just been tricked in a tug o' war game. They shrieked and yelled for what seemed like an hour, but could only have been seconds, as they tried to summon the Winstead sisters.

The pair streaked out of the water, up the banks, and ran as fast as they'd ever run in their lives, across the Strickland farm, past the Brantley house, not stopping until they reached the far field of the Winstead farm. Between fright and gasps of air and pounding hearts they yelled to James Joshua Winstead that his daughters had all gone down into the Indian Hole.

• • •

Right across the property line that separates my yard from that of my parents, is an old family cemetery. But it's not our cemetery. There is a gorgeous gum tree in the center that must be a hundred years old or more. Only one stone is still visible after years of erosion, a stone with the name Dola Winstead. I don't know who she was, and the cemetery has not had a visitor in over half a century.

I remember around the same time I heard all those creaks in the house, there used to be three small metal markers on a long mound just behind Dola's marble marker. They each read "Winstead Daughter," and nothing else. I heard many variations of who was buried there. The local farmhands who helped my folks grow tobacco all seemed to know something about the graves. While none of the stories matched, each contained a variation of the legend of the Indian Hole.

You won't find a definition on Wikipedia or urban legend sources of what an Indian Hole is, or why it is called that. In the 1970s, the old timers on my road described it as an underwater whirlpool or vortex, somehow involving the currents and the effects of the old mill upstream, all of which was compounded by an Indian curse/burial ground/ghost who would wait for white people to come into the water and pull them under. The threat of accidentally stepping into this trap, coupled with the physical evidence of three graves, kept many children out of the Tar River in the Ferrells Township of Nash County. There has not been another reported drowning in the Indian Hole for generations, not since that awful afternoon in 1931.

• • •

It did not take the men of the community long to find the bodies of the Winstead sisters. After they disappeared out of sight completely, the Tar River decided to give the girls back, unmarked, lifeless, along the opposite bank half a mile downstream. Had someone walked upon the scene not knowing the tragedy that had taken place earlier in the day, he might have thought the girls were napping or drying off in the sun, save for the awkward, facedown posture.

Josh Winstead, 56, was no stranger to loss. A widower, he had seen more than his share of heartache. Josh's friends and neighbors helped him make arrangements without delay — in part due to the grievous circumstances, in part due to the oppressive weather and the lack of embalming services available in the area.

On July 4th, while the rest of the country was celebrating 155 years of independence from Great Britain, friends and family and neighbors and curiosity seekers from miles around gathered under a pecan tree just a few feet from the front door in the yard of the Winstead home. Three horse drawn wagons each carried a pine coffin — two of standard size, and one considerably smaller.

The local preacher, who served several congregations in the area, seized the opportunity in front of his largest audience ever, and spoke not just of the tragedy, but also of how the girls were now home in Gloryland with the family they had missed for so long; how in the horror of such an event, the sisters had stuck together to the end, each trying to save the other; and how every God-fearing person should know each day could be his or her last. He was red-faced, and the sweat poured off his bald head.

When he was done, the horses slowly plodded the short distance from the yard to the gum tree where three graves had been dug by lantern light the night before. Eula Pearl, Mamie Harriet and Mary Frances' brothers, Sidney and James, along with a couple of cousins, lowered the boxes into the ground. Neighbors insisted on finishing the job while the surviving Winsteads retreated back to the small, white clapboard house to receive condolences and bowls of food from everyone up and down the road, all the way from Samaria to Spring Hope, five miles away.

There was no mention in the local newspapers of the events, but the Associated Press had a stringer there and reports appeared on front pages of papers all over the South. THREE SISTERS DROWN IN RIVER WHIRLPOOL was the common headline in papers such as *The Tuscaloosa (AL) News*. Most accounts mentioned only Josh by name, containing the horror to just a few lines.

Lottie and Juanita nearly passed out during the funeral and had to be taken back home. Effie, still sick, did not go, but Mr. Burt watched from his front porch, close enough to see but not hear.

• • •

The cemetery was a fixture in the middle of our tobacco field when I was growing up, but none of us gave it much thought. My folks had bought the property from a family named Bryant, back in 1957, so I figured it was some of their kinfolks. For 43 years, I never knew that I had grown up on the old Winstead farm and lived in the same house as those girls. It came up in 2012, when I was talking to Mama about her yard.

"I still miss those trees," Mama said, referring to the two old pecan trees that had been uprooted by Hurricane Fran in 1996. "This place still doesn't look the same."

"Yeah," I said, "I remember riding my bike around that one in the front yard. I built all kinds of roads for my Matchbox cars around the roots."

"They were mighty old," Mama said. "You know, they were old when they had the funeral for those girls under it. Lottie never stopped talking about that, about being there. And poor Mr. Burt ..."

Lottie married a second-generation Lebanese immigrant and her and her husband "Book" were my parents' best friends. Lottie was like family. Her only child was grown, but not married, and I suppose I was a surrogate grandchild. She was a sweet, kind, and loving lady. I think now, that even when she joked, she still had a sadness lingering behind those sparkling eyes. A brain tumor took her before she reached 60.

Mr. Burt was another beloved neighbor to my folks, but Mama said he was never the same after the drowning. His various maladies, real and imagined, treated and untreated, had already made him a melancholy sort. He must have felt some sort of guilt by not making sure those girls went home, but at the same time been so thankful that his Effie had been too sick to go. A couple of weeks after I was born in 1969, when he could see no end to the torment, he sat down on his front porch with his shotgun, stuck the barrel in his mouth and pulled the trigger. He was 75, and had lived with the image of those girls walking away, holding hands, heading towards the Indian Hole, for almost four decades.

• • •

James Joshua "J.J. or Mr. Josh" Winstead lived a hard life. He was born before Custer made his last stand and died before the Japanese bombed Pearl Harbor. He worked his little piece of land, married his sweetheart, Ava Frances Frazier, and started a family. Bettie, the Winstead's first child came along in 1906. Mamie Harriet was born in 1910, Mary Frances in 1913, Sidney in 1916 and then James Herbert in 1918.

On July 1, 1920, Ava gave birth to a stillborn son. It would prove to be a turn in Mr. Josh's life, an irreversible spiral down, a string of events that would make him a tragic figure of Biblical proportions. One bright moment came two years later when Eula Pearl was born. But later that year, another flu epidemic swept the country — this one not as famous, nor with as many casualties as the one in 1918, but it was deadly nonetheless. Bettie, just 16, died on December 22 and Ava followed on Christmas Day, 1922, leaving Mr. Josh with a farm and six mouths to feed, one of whom had yet to turn a year old. He did not re-marry, managing to keep the farm going and the children healthy for almost a decade. Then the drowning happened, leaving him with Sidney and James, who were just 15 and 13 at the time. James would die at 27, and Sidney at 52. Mr. Josh passed away in June 1941, of heart disease. All the neighbors said the doctor was close, but not quite right — it was heartbreak that killed Mr. Josh.

• • •

All children, when they reach a certain age, become alert to sounds in the night, the cacophony of creaks and pops of floorboards, all taking place just beyond the nightlight in the dark. By the time I was in grade school and becoming aware that the world possessed things to be afraid of, most of my siblings had married and moved out, in effect making me an only child.

My room was situated between my parents' room and the kitchen, and my mama would always tell me those sounds were the refrigerator, and my daddy would write every sound off to the house "settling." I couldn't understand why a house never completely settled. I had a hungry imagination, and our house had plenty of creaks and pops to feed it.

After I found out that the Winsteads hadn't lived "close by," they had lived in the house I grew up in, the whole perspective of my childhood fears demanded to be revisited. I thought back to all those times I just knew I heard someone walking through the house; the times I thought I was being watched; the times I was sure I saw shadows in the kitchen, only to have Mama open the door from her room to check on me.

I asked Mama how it was that I lived in a house for 21 years and never knew its history. It just wasn't talked about. Mom tried to let it go at first with a "Oh, I thought all of y'all (meaning my brothers and sisters and me) knew all that stuff." I knew she was holding out, that in a part of the country where fervent religion and curious superstitions manage to somehow co-exist, there had to be more. Surely she had seen or the neighbors had seen three young figures, in the white dresses they supposedly were laid in their coffins wearing, walking across the fields or the path or wandering through the rooms of the house. It would make a good story and make sense as well. My parents had remodeled in 1980, keeping the original core of the house and adding on in a way the girls would not recognize. I wanted to hear that story, the writer in me wanted to tell it, but Mama has always been adamant about the nonexistence of "outright" ghosts, while at other times acknowledging childhood fears of her own regarding "haints." So, even as I pressed, I expected, "Don't be silly." That is where she surprised me.

"No, no, I never saw those girls. But folks used to ask me all the time if I ever heard Mr. Josh walking across the floor at night, back and forth, waiting for those girls to come home. I told them, no, I never heard such a thing. But you know, that house did make a racket creaking at night sometimes."

It did. I wonder if it will ever settle.

• • •

Years ago, they replaced the wooden bridge over the Tar River between my house and Spring Hope. It is concrete and steel girders. It has no character now, but it certainly inspires more confidence. I cross the river every day and at least once a month I think that one day, I'm going to pull on some waders, and walk the banks of the river, the place where it is so narrow, and I'm going to find that Indian Hole. I've been thinking this for years. My brother Bill says he can take me right to it.

There are a multitude of property owners I'd be trespassing against, and way too many folks here and upstream have for some reason decided that the Tar River is a great place to dispose of trash. There are also plenty of illegal and illicit things that go on near the river, involving cash and drugs and I'm sure from time to time, sex as well. I can remember some not so well hidden moonshine stills that were betrayed one year when the leaves came off the trees early.

Those things are reason enough to stay away. After all, no one builds houses on the Tar in this part of the state. It is not pretty, and few have forgotten the flooding wrought by Hurricane Floyd in 1999. There may be fears and superstitions and legends, but I don't really think there is a ghost Indian in the water waiting to drown people. But there is no doubt a danger there, concealed, a killer without conscience or reason. The Winstead sisters are proof of that. I don't have to find the Indian Hole.

• • •

9

Ceasefire

The man in the black and white photo is on one knee. Shadowy, stark, lifeless mountains can be seen in the distance. He has his M1 rifle in one hand, and in the other, a large pheasant. There is a sign to his left that reads "38th Parallel." The foreground is black and flattened. The smile on the man's face is one of pride, and also of joy and satisfaction, the smile of a man who, along with his tent mates, won't be hitting the mess hall or depending on rations — there won't be any "shit on a shingle" tonight. Instead, they will be roasting a delicacy, eating a meal better than they've had for at least a year.

The photo was taken around 1953, almost 20 years before I was born. I'm well acquainted with the man, but still he seems like a stranger. He has short, dark hair, is slender and athletic looking, clean cut and handsome. But what seems out of place is the smile, the posture of confidence. I've never seen *this* man. He is my Daddy.

The man I know has always had white-streaked hair. He's always been to some degree overweight, always with some razor stubble. Smiles most often follow sharp-tongued barbs, profanity, and criticism, sometimes tempered with an off-color expression. The eyes in the photo of a man-boy have been replaced by ones of sadness, despair and regret. Those eyes seldom approved of what I did — from hauling firewood, to schoolwork, to choice of friends, to how much ketchup I used. I joked with my friends that it wasn't until I started playing sports and saw my birth certificate that I realized my name was "Michael," and not "Dammit Michael."

It was many years before I realized that all those things were a result of something that didn't have a name when I was a kid: PTSD.

• • •

I loved to go through the photo albums and boxes of stuff that cataloged my father's time in the U.S. Army. I was fascinated, partly because most of my friends' dads who served in the military were in Vietnam, not Korea. At my nagging, Mama would drag everything out from closets for me, usually over an extended school break during the winter, and let me sift through slides, photographs, insignia, medals, ribbons and postcards.

Daddy was in the 8th Army, and his shoulder patch reads Signal Corps. But there are also medals for marksmanship and sharpshooting. Like most farm boys, he was adept with a rifle, and I had seen his accuracy displayed against livestock predators and agricultural pests.

But I could never get him or Mama to talk to me about Korea. I saw photos of his camp, which always seemed wet and muddy or frozen and piled-high with snow. When I asked about what those days were like, I was told, "Most of the time, I felt like I'd been shot at and missed, and shit at and hit" or that "It was better to be pissed off than pissed on." I once found two sets of insignia, but could get no explanation. I also found a reference to "Sergeant Brantley," but on his discharge papers, it reads Corporal Brantley. I was 40 before Mama ever explained that one.

"I don't remember it exactly," she said. "Your daddy was on guard duty one night, and this colonel and two other officers came out of the officer's club, drunk, in the middle of the night. He got in your daddy's face and started yelling at him to put his cigarette out, because you couldn't smoke on guard duty. Your daddy didn't smoke. So he told the Colonel, 'Sir, it must be the dark, I don't have a cigarette.' So this colonel chewed him out, using every cuss word in the book, threatening your daddy, with this and that and showing off for his friends. Then he tells your daddy he'll have one of his stripes for all that lip." Mama paused on the phone, and I know she is now able to laugh about it. "Well, finally, your daddy says, 'You can have all of my stripes, and shove them up your you-know-what, Colonel You-Know-What, with all due respect, sir.' The colonel's buddies thought it was funny, but your daddy lost a stripe and his pay went back." I knew Mama's smile was gone. At that time, Mama would have been home on the remote farm, away from her family, with an infant son, my oldest brother, Jimmy.

"And, Mr. Bernard at the VA said that was probably the first time that PTSD showed itself."

• • •

It's been called shell shock, combat fatigue, and lots of other names throughout the history of the military. Post-Traumatic Stress Disorder (PTSD) came into use in the 1970s, and was officially recognized in 1980. For a long time, it was mostly associated with Vietnam Veterans, but certainly is not exclusive to them, and has gotten more publicity as a result of the first Gulf War in the early 1990s, and the wars in Afghanistan and Iraq. As it has done shamefully to many who have served our country, the Veterans Administration has been slow to act on this problem, often laying roadblocks of red tape for treatment. Many a veteran has been told "the warehouse with your records burned down." There was apparently an unreported epidemic of fires in the years since World War II. Walk into an American Legion or VFW hall and you'll find someone who has been told that.

Mama has always maintained that Daddy was never the same after he got back from Korea. She said before the draft, he'd never cursed, was easy-going and funny. It was a different story when he returned. The nightmares were frequent, and Mama was often roused from sleep by shrieks of "I'm never going back," "They can't make me go back," or "They should hang all the bastards over there." Korea is known as The Forgotten War, but not by those who were sent there. The war never ended; only a ceasefire was ever signed. To my knowledge, my father has always refused to eat Chinese food, usually saying something to the effect of the last time he ate that 'shit,' there were a million of those SOBs trying to kill him.

After he was discharged, Daddy worked for a defense contractor and then returned to farming. He took a job as manager of a welding supply store not long after that, the first one I remember him having. However, arthritis starting cropping up, and he finally left the working world after a stint at a golf course working the counter and babysitting the poker players hiding from their spouses. His patience seemed to shorten with each change. The severe pain in his joints was often attributed by family doctors to the extreme cold and exposure during his time overseas. However, my folks never considered going to the VA and trying to "get on the dole." They insisted they'd work through it, avoiding the larger issues that were beginning to build.

• • •

I never played catch with my Daddy, never tossed the football. I've never hunted with him, only fished perhaps a handful of times. Most of those activities were delegated to my brother Bill, 10 years older than me. Daddy came home from work, ate the supper Mama usually had on the table, offered a few complaints, flipped through the newspaper and was usually in bed by 7 or 8 p.m.

I can't perform proper maintenance on my cars, repair tractor attachments, spot weld, or build small, outdoor structures with straight edges. My brothers can do all these things. I never seemed to get grass cutting, wood splitting, or any other chore just right. Faced with profanity-singed criticism, as I got older I replied with sarcasm and anger, only feeling remorse after Mama interceded, telling me that Daddy had a rough day, or didn't mean it, or couldn't help it. None of these things comforts an 8 year old or a 16 year old or 40 year old. Mama cooked and cleaned, ran her business and always had a table set, but even she wasn't beyond criticism. From as early as I can remember, I vowed I'd never talk to my sons or wife that way, that I'd never raise my voice in anger.

I did not live with a physically abusive parent or have a tormented childhood. The man never took a drink or a smoke, and no blows were struck between my parents besides quick verbal jabs. Much like Robert Hayden, though, I did fear the chronic angers of that house. I was often guilty of speaking indifferently to him, especially when gruffly ordered to bring in the firewood. His hands ached, and no one thanked him for being a provider; at least I didn't.

Some of my earliest memories are of Sunday afternoons, when my Daddy would take a nap, and I would sometimes climb up on the bed and lie next to him. Without a word, he'd rub my back and tussle my hair and sometimes Mama would join us after she finished cleaning up after lunch. There between the two of them, I knew I was loved. When I look back now, I realize that space was the safest and most secure one on earth.

• • •

I have three children, aged 14, 9 and 7. One night while I was trying to finish a syllabus, return emails and get ready for my first day on my job as a college English instructor, the two youngest, who are boys, turned a small conflict into a full blown professional wrestling match. My daughter intervened with her best attempt at being an adult, but only aggravated the situation. The noise and behavior level deteriorated with each minute. My wife was at a meeting. Finally, I had enough.

"Hey!" I yelled, frustrated after my previous attempts to bring order to the room had been ignored. "Stop this mess, and quit acting like idiots!" I slammed my fist on the arm of the chair, and then clapped my hands loudly. The children froze. I launched into a tirade about behavior, and sent them off to clean up their rooms, chiding them about being spoiled and disrespectful.

The moment I was alone, it felt like smoke burning my eyes and my heart raced. This outburst was not typical of me, and I was embarrassed and fearful. The battles of a career change and financial duress that was nearly three years in the making had manifested themselves in a rage. As a child, I could not understand how someone could act in such a manner, how a man could lose his temper with an innocent child. Then in an instant as an adult, I saw a glimpse of the self I had promised I'd never be. I was shamed. The looks on the faces of my children were probably very much like mine had been 35 years before. I couldn't sleep for two nights, worried, asking myself if this was a beginning.

• • •

Daddy's health declined rapidly in the 90s, and even though he'd always shrugged off doctor visits and taking better care of himself, discovering that he needed immediate open heart surgery for blocked arteries got his attention.

The night before his surgery, everyone gathered at my parents' house to wish him well, comfort him and support Mama. Growing up in the Depression, making it through the Cold War, surviving the farm disasters of the early 1980s, and living in an atmosphere of negativity for so long had hardened her as a pessimist. It was clear that she thought this was it: he would go in for surgery, but probably not come out. Her own father had died from heart problems 30 years before.

A couple of days before that evening, Daddy asked me for a favor. This was unusual. He had handwritten a letter to the family, and he wanted me to type and print copies for everyone. He too thought he was at the end. I offered to photocopy the letter, so it would be in his hand, but he insisted that it be typed, and that if I could, to please make it sound better where it needed to be; fix any spelling errors; and make it sound right. Written by a man I'd never seen take pen to paper, it needed nothing. He apologized for his offenses; praised Mama for how she had raised us, and asked that we all promise him that we would take care of her. He was not pandering or manipulating, he sincerely believed we would be planning his funeral in the next 24 hours. As everyone received copies, a blanket of too-warm sadness enveloped the room, the silence pierced by sniffling. Mama could look at no one, only rest her head in in her palm, arm propped, as she sat on a stool at the kitchen counter.

The surgery was a success. While the letter was sincere, the negativity returned within weeks, and Daddy was not an easy patient. Mama now had new duties, in addition to being the handler — she had to manage medications. It also became clear that depression could no longer be tucked behind the living room recliner. Daddy spent most days in that Barcalounger, taking his meals there, alternating between staring at the television and the ceiling. At the urging of some other veterans, Mama opened a case to get assistance from the VA.

Despite her pragmatism and resolve, Mama had no idea what she would have to go through. They saw countless doctors, went to VA hospitals all over the state, filled out forms, requested records, documented histories. Each time a breakthrough seemed near, some form would suddenly come up missing or some claim would be rejected. Years passed. One administrator brought up PTSD and at least one or two doctors along the way agreed. Finally, things ground to a halt when Mama was informed that all claims had been denied. She told my wife she was out of energy, and that she was going to give up. Kristi urged her not to quit after all the time and energy she had poured into what every doctor agreed was needed. So Mama appealed. The process stalled again until one day when my father had to go fill out more forms. Since he was now using a cane after a couple of falls had resulted in broken hips, she dropped him at the door and parked.

As she made her way into the office, she heard a commotion, a profanity laced tirade, full of rage, a rant so unsettling, it took a moment before she realized it was her husband. After years of having little to say during his appointments, Daddy had reached his breaking point. Mama, flushed with embarrassment, followed the voices and pushed the door to the room open. "What in the world is going on here?" she asked. Daddy immediately shut up and sat down. The administrator seemed unmoved, but looked Mama in the eye and said, "That was the best thing he could have done. There ain't no doubt that man has PTSD." Within weeks, benefits had been approved, retroactive to the date of application years ago.

The Army, which put James Brantley into a situation that would degrade both his mental and physical health for half a century, was now going to throw him a lifeline. While it wouldn't change his disposition, he would be able to afford his medications and pay his bills. It wasn't enough to end his war.

• • •

Daddy did not get better. He developed Type II diabetes. He sometimes refused medications to the point Mama would have to slip them into his food, which we children would joke about during family get-togethers — what was okay to eat, and what was "special." The hurtful comments and criticism of my mother and whomever else came into range continued. Even as I reached my 40th birthday, I had trouble mustering sympathy for any of his inner or outward pains.

Our pastor, a family friend for over 30 years, even pressed me on this.

"You need to have some patience and compassion with your daddy," he told me. "He's in bad shape."

That's easy to say, I replied, but you haven't lived with him.

"You've got to get past all that," he said. "For you and him."

I resented the way I was talked to, but more so the way my Mama was talked to, the toll that had been taken on her for 60 years. My children refer to him as grouchy, and haven't been able to escape his harangues, either. I hate that these will be their memories of him when they become adults. I have the same memory of my grandparents, Daddy's parents, who surely planted those seeds of discontent, unpleasant people in their own right.

I've spent a lot of energy not being my father. I haven't played a whole lot of ball with my kids, but they are young, and we've got time. I coach their sports teams, attend their plays, performances and award ceremonies. I visit their classes and take my turn driving them to school and picking them up. I watch TV with them, talk about vacations or places we will go. I read and tell them stories. I encourage them and tell them I love them every day. I tell them I am proud of them. I don't do this insincerely; I do this because just as a father can show a boy how to be a father by example, he can also show a boy how to be a father by what he doesn't do.

• • •

Not long after the talk with the pastor and the episode with my children, I started feeling bad physically. I don't frequent the doctor, and during the time of my graduate school-career change, we lost our health insurance and have faced some serious financial challenges. There was no longer time for basketball or ice hockey or any other type of exercise. My energy levels fell and my weight ballooned. I developed a kidney stone and then, my doctor wanted to check me for diabetes. I can't rule out depression, but I'm more inclined to think stress. It hit me one day: After a lifetime of running in the other direction, am I turning into my father?

My brothers and sisters all seem to have different memories of Daddy, ones that happened before I came along. Trips, funny stories, long days on the farm. That's when I began to realize that my father's PTSD manifested itself a long time ago. I've never known him when he wasn't fully immersed in the condition — after I was born, it was no longer hinted at, it was pushed to the surface. This realization offered a tiny opening for that compassion the pastor spoke about.

I also remembered things I had not allowed myself to remember. I remember walking into more than one conversation at a family reunion or other function to hear Daddy bragging about newspaper or magazine articles I'd written. When I opened my studio, I could only afford part of the original sign design. The first time I worked out of town and returned, Daddy called the contractor and had the sign finished. I didn't find this out until I called, worried about what I'd be billed for. There were other breadcrumbs sprinkled along the path, ones I'd stepped on or allowed to be eaten by other memories, like crows in our cornfield.

Daddy, now 81, spends most of his days in his chair. He doesn't get out much, and his memory continues to slide along with his health. But when I stop by the house, and it is just Daddy and me, he will ask me questions about my work and chickens. How's the college? Are the chickens laying? He laughs, then forgets. We can talk about stuff in short stretches, before he circles back around to things we've already discussed. He is not like this in small groups; when the house becomes crowded or noisy is when he is at his worst behavior. These are classic signs of PTSD, and it is clear this was the case with him long before any VA doctor said so.

For most of my life, I considered myself without a guiding father figure. I see now I was only willing to look at things from my viewpoint. I never once stopped to think what had been taken from him, the things he saw and experienced that none of his family will ever know the details of, but which shaped all of our lives. Now, there is a ceasefire.

• • •

10

Driving to Florida with Elvis

I remember each rhythmic thump-thump of the tires bringing us closer to Walt Disney World. As each green and white highway sign came into view, I consulted the map my parents let me pick up at a South Carolina rest stop a couple of hours into the trip. It had taken forever to put our little pocket of North Carolina, where the Tar River cuts eastward, far enough into the rear view mirrors that I could no longer see it.

I measured the distance left to Orlando, Florida. As we alternated between sterile I-95 and eclectic U.S. 301, depending on traffic as well as Daddy's inclinations, the blue and white VW van made steady time. When the map got boring, I read the latest issue of *Sport* magazine. There was a pennant race going on. At eight, I had yet to become a New York Yankee hater, instead intrigued by the insanity of manager Billy Martin who I had seen throwing hats and kicking dirt on umpires on TV. Mostly, I was interested in Catfish Hunter. The hard throwing righthander had grown up less than two hours east of us, and was a North Carolina treasure as well as one of the best players in the game.

If that got boring, I had a bag of well-worn "Amazing Spider Man" comics and an assortment of books. When Mama had announced the trip and told me it would be about a 12-hour ride, I had carefully planned out how to fill my time. Daddy had already told me I could not spend the whole 600-mile trip asking questions. I had the middle bench seat all to myself and plenty of room. I could daydream about all the things I'd heard about Disney World and where I wanted to go and that I would finally be getting a pair of those mouse ears like all the kids on the commercials. I figured I'd get them as soon as we got inside the park and wear them all day.

I also had my older sister Jane, who was 18, and her soon-to-be-fiancée, Eddie, behind me in the third seat. While they were giggly and in love and silly, I loved being around both of them. My brother Bill, Jane's twin, had decided that having us in Florida while he was at home alone was too good to pass up.

The van, although relatively new and modern, only had an AM radio. We listened to it on and off, and just before stopping for supper, Mama found a news station. That was when we heard that Elvis Presley had died. Not much was said in the car, but the mood behind me was somber; I could feel it without even turning around. Among the black lights and peace posters, Jane had several black-and-white glossies of the rock and roller tacked on her bedroom walls, and her stash of 8-track tapes was filled with Elvis recordings.

By the time we stopped for supper, and got settled into our hotel room somewhere in Georgia, south of Savannah, Elvis was all over the television and radio. I heard conversations and whispers among every waitress, patron, hotel clerk and person in the lobby, all things I mostly couldn't understand except for the unmistakable words "Graceland," "The King," and "Drugs."

• • •

The one thing I remember, and Mama has confirmed, and Jane and Eddie — now divorced — have independently agreed upon, is what we saw the next day. Every few cities, on the marquee of arenas, we saw

"Concert Cancelled" followed by a specific date, and then usually another line with "RIP Elvis." Despite this being a specific memory for us, a look back at Elvis' August 1977 tour dates show only one (Fayetteville, NC) that would have been on our route, long since passed the day before.

We hit Florida and immediately considered that Florida in the dog days of summer was not ideal. Mama has insisted for years that the trip was a spontaneous decision, and there is no better evidence.

Jane was still down, and it didn't help that every gas station we stopped, every restaurant, and every dial on the radio was playing "Hound Dog," "Jailhouse Rock," "Heartbreak Hotel," or the tear-jerking "My Way." Elvis was no longer Elvis, he was Elvis Aaron Presley. Newscasters on the radio were saying people would remember where they were just like they did when they found out that JFK had been assassinated.

As it turned out, I was much more affected in the fall when Lynyrd Skynyrd had their tragic plane crash that killed three band members. I preferred "Simple Man" and "Sweet Home Alabama" blaring from my brother's room.

· · ·

Our first stop was in Silver Springs, a sort of wild garden/water springs park near Orlando. A glass bottom boat ride seemed to be the big attraction. It was amazing how clear the water was, and the vegetation and wildlife was much different than what we had in eastern North Carolina.

I remember the hanging Spanish moss and seeing my first live alligator. I read recently that with all the parks added by Disney over the years, and the degradation of the springs Silver Springs closed and later became a state park.

By the end of the day, I'd had enough tropical nature. I was ready to see the castle, the one from the opening credits that I watched every Sunday night on the "Wonderful World of Disney." And of course, I wanted my big black mouse ears, the ones with the red and white and sticker featuring Mickey himself.

That night at the Days Inn, Daddy flipped a brochure to me. Eddie grinned and told me he was pretty sure I'd like the next stop. I picked up the glossy color trifold, more than a little aggravated until I saw the name: Six Gun Territory. If there was anything I liked better than Disney, it was the Wild West.

• • •

Elvis' death temporarily bumped another summer sensation out of the headlines. David Berkowitz was arrested and revealed as Son of Sam, the serial killer who murdered six people and wounded seven more in New York from 1976 until his arrest just days before Elvis died.

Berkowitz didn't just terrorize New York City, the nation was on edge. I had relatives and neighbors who were certain that the Son of Sam would soon flee New York and come directly to our county and continue killing. I watched Walter Cronkite every night for updates.

There had been blackouts and rioting in New York, a coup in China, and a devastating flood in West Virginia. It was a crazy summer. At the time, I thought maybe I was getting the vacation of a lifetime, going to Walt Disney World. Looking back now, I wonder if maybe Mama and Daddy didn't need to escape the real world, one that seemed on fire.

• • •

Eddie had introduced me to Clint Eastwood's spaghetti westerns. I watched reruns of "The Wild, Wild West." Saturday afternoons often meant "Bonanza" or "Gunsmoke." My brother Bill was hooked on "Kung Fu," which featured a main character that was Bruce Lee made into a cowboy.

I'd never heard of Six Gun Territory, but it was spectacular. We walked through the gate, which set my parents back less than $30 for the lot of us, and I was instantly in awe. Laid out before me was a complete Western town, forty buildings in all. The streets were dirt, there were hitching posts, horses, bad guys in black hats, the sheriff's office, wagons, a saloon and a hotel.

We walked around for a bit, me in short cotton athletic shorts, a t-shirt and tube socks with stripped tops (the photographs from the trip still make me cringe). There was a sense that something was going down soon. Shady characters with holstered pistols gave us the eye, the deputies kept a wary lookout. We ducked into the Palace Saloon for an order of cold Coca-Colas and by the time we found a seat, a group of dance hall girls in low cut, red and black dresses, high heels and black stockings took the stage. They high-stepped and lifted their skirts frequently. Daddy and Eddie enjoyed it immensely and the place rocked with laughter. When the routine was over, the women dispersed into the crowd for photographs with patrons. I turned my attention to my Coke and when I looked up, Eddie had a girl on each knee and a giant grin, encouraging Mama to get a picture. Suddenly realizing I was at the table, one of the women took her boa and ran it across my face.

"Hey fella, you got a girlfriend back home?"

I felt the heat rush to my face and Eddie and Jane howled. The showgirl looked a lot different up close than she had under the stage lights. She was heavily made up, so much so that Daddy remarked later that it would take a belt sander to get it off at night. She looked much older and tired, but it didn't matter, I was smitten.

My infatuation didn't last long, however, as a townsperson/character rushed into the saloon shouting that there was trouble out on the street and we should rush out to the sidewalk to see what was sure to be an impending shootout. I hit the swinging doors just in time to hear shouting and fist shaking, between the clean cut men with badges and the scraggly attired bad guys. The next thing I knew, there was quick drawing and gun shots and a man fell off of a nearby roof. My heart raced. Another grabbed his chest and slumped into the water trough. The battle continued until the sheriff made his move and shot down the leader of the bad guys, a man in a black hat.

After the dust cleared, we made our way around the park. I remember riding the train, but my mind was still on the gunfight. I didn't think much about Disney World, as I now had my sights set on something completely different. The gift shop had a pair of faux-ivory handle imitation Colt revolver cap guns, the kind that took a load of half-inch thick red paper caps with small, gunpowder-filled blisters. The tape fed through the middle of the gun up through the hammer. The pistols made a very authentic sound, and the smell of spent gunpowder with a little wisp of smoke was just too much to resist.

I played with those guns the rest of the trip, to the point my parents threatened to confiscate them. They were my favorite toys for a long time, and I won lots of shootouts under the pecan trees when I got back home. When I got married and moved out of my parents' house, those six-shooters were still in use, floating loose in the toy box Mama used to entertain her grandchildren.

• • •

Baseball was interesting that summer, in particular the fortunes of the New York Yankees. Despite the location and team name, the Yankees were extremely popular in North Carolina, mostly because of Jim "Catfish" Hunter. Hunter was from the northeastern corner of the state, near Edenton. He was successful with the Oakland A's, winning World Series in 1972, 1973 and 1974 as well as the Cy Young award that last season as the best pitcher in the American League. He became a household name the next year when he signed the richest free agent contract in baseball history, and delivered 23 wins for the Yankees. The following year, he won 17, and then tailed off to just 21 wins over the next two seasons, but New York won two World Series titles.

Not long after that, I managed to pull off a three-way trade with my friends Kevin and Andy, one that landed me a 1979 Topps baseball card of Hunter in his Yankee uniform. I gave up an older card that featured

Reggie Jackson and Pete Rose.

Years later, when I worked for newspapers, I had the chance to meet Hunter when he coached his son's American Legion team. It was then I realized that despite the grizzled look he sported on his trading cards and in those World Series battles on TV, the man had retired as a 200-game winner, was a multi-millionaire at the ripe old age of 33, and a Hall of Famer by the time he turned 41.

· · ·

I could have spent more time at Six Gun Territory, and I regret my boys will never get to experience it. Less than a decade after our visit, it was bulldozed and eventually replaced with Six Gun Plaza. The park became another casualty of the Walt Disney World entertainment behemoth.

Disney is one of those rare places that lives up to the hype, the buildup, the expectations. And mine were high that hot summer day in August. After the car ride and the hotels and the meals out and the other stops on our tour, I was wide open. We rode the monorail and we took the train around the park. My family was not scary-ride people, we liked other attractions. I had to be pulled out of the fort in Frontier Land, as I surveyed the park from the ramparts and the watchtower. The view was surpassed only by the Swiss Family Robinson Tree House.

We did the Haunted Mansion, the Hall of Presidents, the Mississippi River Boat Ride, Tomorrow Land and some kind of magic carpet trip around the world in the 360-degree view theater. Mama and Jane were entranced by "It's a Small World After All," and we went through the line at least twice, the refrain of the song sticking in our brain for days, bringing jokes each time. Daddy did not go on many rides, often saying he would wait for us on a bench, only to be found right in front of an ice cream stand each time, tipping a vanilla cone at us as we exited. He seemed happy, free of home, free of the stresses of the farm and his job, free of the arthritis which would nearly cripple him, and with no signs of what we'd later come to know as PTSD.

As the day spiraled to an end, so did I. We secured a nice spot near the castle to watch the fireworks and we could hear the shrieks from some of the rides, as well as the sword fight from the pirate ship. Just a year removed from the Bicentennial, the Disney fireworks show put to shame anything we had experienced previously. We were mesmerized and said nothing. We all stood with our necks craned to the sky, watching the shells climb and explode in a kaleidoscope of colors.

And then we had a moment that has become more solidly fixed in our memories as the one thing that everyone names first about that trip. Only my family could spend an incredible day in the most famous amusement park in the world and take home a scene of total and complete disaster for a young dad as a favorite memory.

When the fireworks ended, we were ill-prepared for the near-panicked exit of the patrons for the monorail and the trolleys to the parking lot. It was as if people thought that if they dallied just a bit, they would trapped in the fantasy land. Suddenly, a man pushing a baby stroller emerged from a cluster of people, apparently either trying to cut a path for his wife and child or find them, as the stroller was empty except for a large diaper bag. He then ran roughshod through the street, clipped some people in the legs, ran over toes and forced those alert enough to see him coming to jump out of the way. Had this been the day before, I'm sure the sheriff would have shot him, or at least arrested him in good order at Six Gun Territory. As he bore down on us, he showed no signs of slowing down for the curb of Main Street USA.

We watched as the man must have thought his stroller would hit the curb and pop over the top, sort of like a monster truck. Instead, the stroller hit the curb and literally disintegrated, blown apart into what must have been a dozen pieces. The man, no longer able to rely on speed for balance, went tumbling. The folks in his wake clapped, while my family laughed hysterically.

• • •

The world wouldn't be the same when we returned to Nash County. In short order, there would be Apple computers and Atari video games. Eddie and Jane got married, and Eddie took me to see "Star Wars" and "Raiders of the Lost Ark" and I started to grow up. But that summer, I thought things would never change and that was just fine with me. I never did get my Mickey Mouse ears.

• • •

11

Rationed

War Ration Book No. 3, serial number 747986, despite bearing my Daddy's name in pencil, is, according to the WARNING clearly printed on the cover, property of the United States government.

Roughly the same dimensions of a postcard, the booklet has yellowed with age, peeling back and softening at the corners. It was issued in the fall of 1943, when Daddy was 10 years old. He must have thought it was a really neat to have a book of stamps that featured illustrations of a field artillery piece, a tank, an aircraft carrier and a fighter plane. Most of the stamps are still intact, despite the shortages then of many goods. I've asked him about this over the years, and in particular what store his family patronized.

"Grocery store? We didn't go to the grocery store. We grew everything."

"Sugar? Gas? Coffee? You had to get some things from the store."

When I was younger, this would often be followed by the pat answer: "Don't be such a smartass." But lately, as Daddy's health continues to decline, his face goes blank, strained, as he searches for memories that are either no longer there, or are buried so deeply in the warehouses of his mind they can't be found.

• • •

About once a week after supper, when I was in elementary school, we visited my grandparents. Daddy grew up in a century-old, two-story, white house, surrounded by sheds and packhouses of farm equipment, seed, fertilizer, pastures of cows and bordered by the Tar River, 35 miles east of Raleigh. It was a house his daddy bought at auction, moving the family from the humble homeplace a few miles away.

My paternal grandparents were as ancient to me as the house, and even as a seven-year old, the thought that my grandmother was born in the 1800s seemed impossible. She was old enough to remember Teddy Roosevelt as a Rough Rider, and at 21, not having yet married my grandfather, was considered an old maid when the Titanic sank. My grandfather, a decade younger than her, predated the Wright brothers' flight. I remember they were gray-white, grouchy and immobile; she in a wheelchair, and he hobbled from toes lost to diabetes. They let me and my parents know that children were best seen and not heard, and that I could most certainly benefit from less sparing of the rod.

I dreaded the visits because their house was always hot, and smelled funny — an odd mix of musty stuffiness, pipe smoke, greasy food and bug spray. There wasn't anything to do but listen to gossipy complaints. Mama always looked miserable as well.

My refuge was Mrs. Whitley. She was nearly as old as my grandparents and rented a road-front bungalow on the farm. Her home had an entirely different atmosphere. Throughout the house and covering nearly every inch of her screened-porch were dozens of terra cotta pots, planters, hanging baskets, glass bottles, and moonshine jugs, each with plants from the mundane to the exotic. Damaged aquariums were converted into terrariums. Mrs. Whitley was always welcoming, wearing a homemade dress, stockings, dress shoes and horn-rimmed glasses on a beaded chain. Her hands were dry and aged, but her touch on my shoulder when I arrived, and the hugs when I left were as soft and warm as my bed sheets when Mama brought them in from the clothesline on a hot July day.

I'd run to her screen door and yell for her. She was almost always tending her plants on the front porch. She'd call me by my full name, invite me to come on in and help her "water up." She showed me the wonders of the aloe plant, which she called a "medicine plant," the amazing Venus flytraps, geraniums that she could make bloom all year and all types of ferns. She showed me seed trays of the latest things she started and how to look for bugs and diseases.

Once we had worked our way through the house, she'd pull an ice cold, glass bottle of 7-Up out of her refrigerator and ask me to split it with her while we talked about what cuttings she would send me home with, and how to make sure they grew. We talked about school and books and farming and sat on her porch in rockers, watching the cars zip by on the highway just a few yards away as Alex Trebek read answers on Jeopardy, blaring from the small black and white Zenith in the living room. Sometimes we talked about her late husband, or her kids or grandkids.

Even in the hot July summers, that porch was nice and cool. Sometimes we got out her electric ice crusher, dumped cubes from the old metal-levered ice trays into the hopper and ground away on a contraption that was as loud as a chainsaw. The 7-Up was always better served that way.

When Mama came to get me, she'd always ask if I had been good. Oh, he's such a sweet boy and a big helper, he can come over anytime, Mrs. Whitley said with a big smile, even though I know I had to wear her out some evenings with all my questions.

Her house was comfortable and friendly and safe. I didn't have to sit and be quiet. I never ride by that old house — long empty — without thinking about those summer evenings, and I've never seen an aloe plant as big as those Mrs. Whitley grew.

• • •

This book is valuable. Do not lose it. That is the first instruction listed on the back of War Ration Book No. 3. There are other instructions as well, indicating that the enclosed stamps would be required, in addition to money, to buy rationed goods and that time, place, quantity and cost would be established by the Office of Price Administration. Unused books were not to be thrown away, even after they expired.

The instructions are followed by a good bit of propaganda. Rationing was vital to the war effort and any attempt to violate the rules was an "effort to deny someone his share and will create hardship and help the enemy." A ration book was the government's "assurance of your right to buy your fair share of certain goods made scarce by the war." Price ceilings were set to contain inflation, and consumers were advised to not pay more than posted prices. Finally, there was an admonition, "If you don't need it, don't buy it."

The front cover was to include the vital entry of identification information such as the address, height, weight, age and sex of the holder, as well as the occupation. Only Daddy's name, James, is entered, by my grandmother's hand, writing so distinctive that I recognize it even though I only knew the woman for nine years.

There is one final warning on the booklet. Violators of rationing rules were subject to a $10,000 fine, which today is the equivalent of $136,000.

• • •

The tide of World War II was turning in 1943. By the time Daddy's family received War Ration Book No. 3, Italy had been invaded, and within a month Marines were on Tarawa. FDR, Churchill, and Stalin were already talking about Operation Overlord.

Times were tough on the home front. Income tax rates ranged from 81-94 percent, and workers were constantly encouraged to buy war bonds. Women and teenagers took on many jobs previously held only by men. Nearly 300,000 Mexican laborers were brought in by the government to work on farms. None of them went to the farm outside where five people depended on it to survive — my grandparents, headed past middle age, Daddy, and his two brothers.

• • •

Rationing was like most government programs — wrought with complications, filled with exemptions for powerful people and ripe for corruption.

There were several parts to the rationing program. There was uniform rationing, which provided equal shares of a single commodity, such as sugar. Point rationing was for processed foods such as meat and cheese, and differential rationing of things such as gas and fuel oil depending on need. Other items fell under certificate rationing, which required citizens to provide an application and demonstrate a need for such items as tires, cars, stoves and typewriters.

Prices were posted in stores, but it's hard to find prices because the combination of stamps required varied from the issue of each price list, which was determined by supply and demand. Another complication was that the buyer not only had to have stamps, he or she had to have the cash money to make the purchase as well. No change was given until books were issued in 1944 that featured ration coins, red and blue paper circles about the size of a dime.

Vehicles required one of five types of stickers on the front windshield. A Type-A black sticker was the most common, which allowed the holder to buy four gallons of fuel per week. "Pleasure riding" was strictly forbidden. A Type-B green sticker was issued for driving essential to the war effort and allowed the purchase of eight gallons per week. Red Type-C stickers were for doctors, ministers, mailmen and railroad workers, and T stickers were for truckers. Members of Congress and other VIPs were given Type-X stickers, which carried no restrictions.

Despite the warnings of penalties and fines and unpatriotic behavior, an entire underground industry based around ration books developed. There was fraud, forgery and theft of books, as well as an exchange system of cash for certain high demand stamps and hoarding of goods for sale at a later time. A black market arose almost immediately upon commencement of the program.

My parents remember a more common gray market that developed among neighbors and was common in rural areas. Mama's family of six, all with a weakness for sweets, always ran through their allotment of sugar, so they swapped stamps with friends and family who needed other things. In their estimation, each person legitimately issued a book of stamps was entitled to use all of the stamps. No one was stealing or acquiring extra books, they all simply had different grocery lists.

The government tried to combat this by stipulating that clerks remove stamps from intact books presented at purchase. This was practically impossible to enforce, and as long as the number of stamps matched the inventory sold, there was no problem.

• • •

I feel guilty sometimes that I didn't make more of an effort to be a better grandchild to Daddy's parents. I always excuse myself by thinking that I was just a child, and that they should have been kinder and gentler with me. I wonder how Daddy's childhood must have been, how it was to have love rationed.

Not long after my grandmother died, my grandfather passed, before I even made it to middle school. When Daddy and his older brother had to sort and distribute belongings, I made the trek up the wide, grand, polished, wooden staircase. It was known that the house was so carefully and skillfully crafted, that in many places it is held together by pegs rather than nails. I never went upstairs when my grandparents were alive, so for me, it was a lifting of the veil. The second floor was right out of a Hitchcock film, furniture covered in white sheets, large empty rooms, wonderful views of pastures and even a glimpse of the river in winter, when the leaves were off the trees. I wonder if my grandparents were a reflection of the house, the best parts covered, hidden, long forgotten, but full of small treasures. They spent most of their time in just three rooms, rarely enjoying what they had, mostly griping when I was around.

I helped with the cleanup and my fascination with history was piqued at every turn. On a desk, much like the one where I pay bills now, stacked as if waiting for immediate attention, were the ration books. There are plenty left for gasoline, sugar and other staples. There were whole newspapers lying around, waiting to be read, from the day after events such as Pearl Harbor. It was as if those incidents had happened that week, not 40 years earlier. I also found an old schoolbook. It belonged to my grandfather a man who always seemed so humorless, but who inscribed an old saw he scribbled on the leaf cover:

Do not steal this book my friend,
For fear the gallows will be your end.
And when you hear your long neck crack,
You'll wish I had my book back.

I rescued these items from disposal and they have a place in my home and imagination. I don't know what memories my children will retain and what will be discarded in their minds, although I fear his PTSD from another war, Korea, has entrenched Daddy as a grumpy old man to them. As parents, my wife and I think, "They'll always remember this." But I see the fallacy of this, as I listen to the things they talk about and the things I overhear them tell other people. It is interesting what sticks with us, the things we tuck away into a book of memory all our own, and savor like a cool 7up over crushed ice on a screened porch in the summer.

• • •

12

Two Minutes for Roughing

We were walking the concourse during an NHL intermission in Raleigh, NC. There was a piece of 8 ½ x 11 copy paper, held to the wall with masking tape near one of the concession stands.

"Learn to Play Hockey," it read. "All Ages Welcome. No equipment needed. Sunday Nights. 6-7 p.m." I looked at my best friend John. "I'm in if you are," I said. Immediately, John said, "Let's do it." We'd made a lot of decisions this way, and many had ended poorly. The was the time we got "pulled" while kayaking on the Bogue Sound by a game warden, on suspicion of "poaching and boating while impaired;" taunted an NHL enforcer mercilessly to the point he tried to climb the glass to get to us in the stands; the fireworks debacle of New Year's Eve 2001; and turning a church paintball outing into a scene from "Apocalypse Now."

It was exciting that first night we sat in the locker room and tried to figure out how to strap on shoulder and chest pads, elbow pads, shin guards, helmets, gloves and all the other pieces. Skates had to be tight, but not too tight. Hockey pants had to give here, but not slip there. Balance and center of weight were the keys to this puzzle.

• • •

It was a job that needed doing, and my wife had just reminded me that my next day off would be a great time to get after it: cleaning out my "man closet." This was the warehouse for the sports card collections and comic books of my youth, old toys, golf clubs and accumulated sports memorabilia.

Near the bottom shelf, I found my Bauer ice skates. These were no ordinary skates, and couldn't be bought in this configuration from a pro shop. The black and white boots had once belonged to Carolina Hurricanes forward Josef Vacisek, a sometimes awkward forward with a deft wrist shot, and, like me, a size 11. I paid $75 for the skates at the team's annual equipment sale. A custom pair would have run about $350 new. Black Sharpie scribbles on the blade guard listed Vasicek's jersey number and the last time of sharpening, 9-17-02.

Vasicek wasn't the best player on the team, he was a big guy, a role player who always played hard. I liked that, and could certainly identify with it throughout my modest athletic career. I had a chance to meet him once at a team event, and he was a nice guy who laughed when I told him I was putting his old blades to use. After playing out the string in the NHL, he spent some time in Europe, and I remember the sadness I felt when I heard that he and most of his teammates had died in a plane crash in Russia a few years ago.

The skates the pros wear have a better fit, and added protection against 100mph slapshots and the inevitable violence that occurs when men opposing each other are armed with sticks. The laces were in good shape and the blades still fairly sharp. My lace puller, a pocket knife-sized tool that helps get the boot tight, was tucked in the heel. Beaten and dinged all around, the skates were still more than serviceable. I could relate to that, too. A faint smell of locker room wafted up when I pulled the tongue forward, and it took me back.

• • •

Gene was our instructor. He was a congenial and patient former minor league player with hair as white as the ice — until he took a week off. The next class, he showed up with coal black hair, so black it had a weird sheen to it.

"Man, does Gene look weird to you?" John asked.

"You mean because his hair is a color that doesn't exist in nature?" I replied.

"What color do you call that? If you look at it from different angles, it changes." From that moment on, we referred to our instructor as "Just for Men" Gene.

By the last day of class, John had become a pretty good skater, with no shot. I could barely move, but had a pretty decent wrist shot. Just For Men Gene declared us all ready for the Beer League draft, lied when he said we'd do well, and skated off the ice for a date with his new girlfriend, who was still in the cradle when he retired.

• • •

I loved Paul from the moment I played my first shift. As I headed up the ice on a possession change, a player hooked my skates from behind and yanked my feet out from under me, laughed and skated away. At the end of my shift, I went to the bench furious. Hockey is a fast sport and the play came back down to our end of the ice quickly. When the guy who tripped me set up in front of the goal, Paul immediately gave him a two-handed crosscheck to the upper back, crumpling him to the ice.

Paul had a fierce temper. He was constantly getting in scrums with opposing players. If the officials didn't dispense justice as he saw fit, Paul took things into his own hands. He was the guy you wanted on your team, but hated to play against.

• • •

Beer League drafts — the method in which players are assigned to teams — are not given deep thought by rink officials. New teams that don't have enough players, get all the guys right out of Learn to Play.

After two years, John and I became captains of our own team. We brought over some guys from our previous team and took what the league director gave us to fill out the roster. Two guys showed up with their gear still in plastic wrap.

We got beat badly that first season as the Jackals. The league director couldn't even spell our team name correctly. In a sport where games are often 5-3 or 4-2, we lost 9-1 and 10-3. Our goalie, who should have never seen more than 30 shots in our 45 minute games, saw as many as 73 shots a night. Ian got about three years' worth of experience in three months, but never complained. "The good news is, at least I didn't have time to get bored like the other team's goalie," he'd often say.

Instead of discouraging us, those losses forged a bond. Some teams fussed and argued among themselves, even when they were winning. Not the Jackals.

There is basically no sportsmanship in Beer League hockey. Teams run up the score and talk trash. So, we started taking penalties. Hard ones. We had roughnecks and rednecks and probably a chemical imbalance of testosterone. We quickly found out that more talented opponents don't like physical play. Our motto became, "We might get beat, but we don't get beat up." The beauty of hockey is an unspoken rule that players police themselves. If someone is taking cheap shots, the refs will often let it go until the victim, or one of his teammates, decides enough is enough and retaliates. The refs usually let this go as well. When penalties are called, they are not severe: you have to go sit in a box, by yourself, for two minutes, and do nothing. A smart player knows to do this right at the end of a 2-minute shift, when he is already tired and going to the bench anyway. In Beer League, power plays don't make much difference.

• • •

Bruce turned physical play into a work of art. He looked and played like one of the Hanson brothers from the movie *Slapshot* — he sported horn-rimmed glasses, held together with white tape in the middle.

Bruce was a chemist at a company in the Research Triangle Park. His company made a drug that made the news one week after three people died from taking it. He wore a t-shirt promoting the drug under his uniform the next game.

"What the hell, Bruce?" Jonah asked when he saw the shirt.

"Damnit," Bruce said, "you have a drug that makes 4,997 people get better and three people die and it's a scandal. People die, man. They were already sick."

He had a knack for working guys over so discreetly during a game, an opponent would sometimes attack him. He always came to the bench smiling. Someone would always ask what happened.

"I slashed him in the nuts," Bruce said. "But he's a shit and had it coming."

• • •

Eventually, we started winning some games. We were having fun and getting better. At a captain's meeting one night, the league director told the group, that if he was playing in our league, he would want to be a Jackal. "Those guys have fun," he said, while pointing at John and me, "and don't bitch at each other."

We still had some tough times. One night, we were up against a really good team. A laser shot came at Ian, it hit the goalpost, bounced straight back to another player who rocketed it into the back of the goal. Ian acted like nothing had happened. We were already down four goals and I saw a chance to salvage some fun.

"Holy crap, can you believe that?" I asked the ref.

He looked at me blankly while the other team celebrated.

"That guy shot that thing so hard it hit the boards and came back through that hole in the net," I said. "You see the hole, right?"

The ref looked down. "Yeah?" he said.

There was no hole.

"What a shot," Ian said. "You couldn't even see it."

I piled it on. "It flew right over the crossbar and took that weird angle. Man, what a shot. But you know, it never went in the front of the goal."

The ref nodded. "That IS a small hole," he said. "They should fix that." He raised his arms, crossed them, and waved off the goal. I got off the ice, as the other teams' captains skated over, enraged, cursing, furious at being denied an obvious score. The shouting only ended when the official threatened to start handing out unsportsmanlike penalties.

John, who was on the bench, told me on the ride home that the guys on the bench couldn't figure out what I was doing. "They were all saying, 'What the hell could he be talking to the ref about?' and I just told them to just enjoy it."

• • •

Behind my skates, on a shelf, I found my helmet. It was clear with a plexiglass face shield and air holes around the jaw. When I grabbed it, a piece of the hard foam padding from the right earhole fell on the floor. It was yellow with age and what must have been gallons of sweat that soaked in over the years. Hockey, even when played poorly and with little skill, is a great workout.

What I'd never noticed was the wear and tear on the black outer shell. There were scars and scrapes and scuffs all around, from hits, falls, deflected pucks and errant stick blades. But there was one in particular, a peeling of plastic like that on skin you can get from bare legs or arms meeting wire fencing, sea shells, fish hooks, thorns or broken glass, that was worse than the others. While the other marks had become part of an anonymous group, I knew exactly when this gash was made.

One night, after a stoppage in play, a guy skated by me for the next faceoff and slashed me across the legs, while yelling at me. I had no idea what had brought this on, so I responded by doing the same to him.

When I turned my back, he used his stick to hit me in the helmet. Something changed in that split second when my head snapped violently to the side. The sound was turned off. I saw the referee who was right beside my assailant and me, and I noticed for the first time my attacker had about three inches of height advantage and more bulk. My reaction was quick — I punched him as hard as I could right in the mouth. He wasn't wearing a facemask, and he lost his helmet. He reached to grab my arm to pin me for a sucker punch, but rage took over. I picked him up and slammed him to the ice and I threw one right hand after the other. The sound returned, and I heard the officials yelling at somebody to stop punching. While punching the guy in the face, I started yelling — for reasons still unknown to me — "I'm not punching him!"

The instant they pulled me off, I regretted everything that had just happened. Who was the angry person? My teammates were going nuts on the bench. The referees huddled. I told one that I surely hoped that guy would get thrown out for hitting me in the head and then throwing punches. They sent me to the penalty box while they sorted things out.

After about five minutes the verdict was in: I got two minutes for roughing and two minutes for unsportsmanlike conduct. He got two minutes for roughing, two minutes for unsportsmanlike, and 10 minutes for fighting, which carried an automatic ejection and league suspension. From that moment on, that game was known as "the night Brantley went nuts."

• • •

In hockey, they say goalies have to be a little weird. They have to be to stand around and let other men use high tech composite sticks to fire a frozen piece of vulcanized rubber at them. Ian was no exception.

He drank anywhere from one to three Red Bulls before every game. He wrote messages to the other team on his stick. An art teacher by day, he often arrived early to our games to leave homemade fliers in the opposing team's locker room, offering final score predictions. We only discovered this one night when we found a stray one on the floor of the lobby.

Goalie is a position that often gets no loyalty from team captains. As teams get better or get close to the top of the league, they will often jettison a goalie for a better one. Ian gave up a lot of goals in the early days, but he saw an insane amount of shots. He never got mad at our bone-headed defensive plays, never complained and never quit. He played hurt, and he got darn good from seeing all those shots, stealing games for us and playing his best hockey in both championships.

We never once considered replacing him.

• • •

Our team had conservatives, liberals, corporate managers, chemists, religious guys, hedonistic guys, Yankees, Southerners, immigrants, young guys, old guys and everything in between.

We had arguments, questioned each other's manhood, passed gas, threatened to pass gas, had wardrobe malfunctions, had awkward moments of nakedness, got mad and got over it.

During timeouts, we didn't talk strategy, we confirmed who brought the beer, or we told stupid jokes. One night, we were down by four goals going into the last period. I called timeout and gathered everyone around the bench.

"Men, I've got something to say," I started. Eyes rolled and there was cursing; they knew my "Animal House" speech was coming. "We might be down four goals, but we're not quitters. Did we quit when the Germans bombed Pearl Harbor? No! And we're not going to quit now. Who's with me?" I looked down the bench at each guy on the team, with my arms spread apart like a TV evangelist.

The whistle blew and I looked at the other bench. The captain was furiously scribbling plays on a dry erase clipboard. Our guys climbed over the boards, shaking their heads. We scored five goals in 15 minutes to win the game.

. . .

There were five guys on our team named Chris. We called them all by their last names. Sakell was very serious, and always looked mad, even when he was having fun. Manaro was a new guy we had wanted to join the team. On his first night, Jonah wanted to discuss what was apparently a sex cult he had discovered on the Internet. Testa was volatile — he might rip a bathroom door off the hinges in a fit of rage, and then turn around and tell a joke. Creed never seemed to know what to make of all the big personalities. Wright's (not his real name) marriage came apart one season and he fell into a bad place, dating strippers and adult film stars.

. . .

A spectator only had to watch for a few minutes to see we were not the most talented team in the Beer League. Not even close. It seemed every team had more talent.

But we had brains. Or at least we thought we did — and sometimes that is all that matters. We had a chip on our shoulder, shaped and molded by losses and perceived disrespect. So we used psychological warfare.

Whenever I talked to a ref, I tried to make sure I was out of hearing range of players on the other team, and I'd always try to point in another player's direction, or at something just past him. This drove guys crazy. If the referee looked, or I could get him to point, it was all the better.

A ref once told John and me that he knew we played head games. We thanked him. "I didn't mean that as a compliment," he said. So, we thanked him again, repeatedly, and told him what a great job he was doing, even if the opposing captain had said he sucked as a ref. "Dammit, you guys are doing it right now."

• • •

Vlad was from Russia. Martin was from Sweden. J.B. was from France. Pat was from Canada. Each one fit in perfectly.

J.B. took a lot of heat over being French, especially when "Freedom Fries" and French jokes were in plentiful supply. He just rolled with it. Martin, the most talented player I've ever seen, never got completely comfortable in our locker room. His European manners were in conflict with the teasing and tormenting. Sometimes, he seemed agitated on the bench. One night, I asked him what was wrong.

"Ah, hmm. We don't joke so much in Sweden. Sweden is very serious. When you guys said you all wanted to go to Sweden over Christmas, I told my mother my team wanted to come. She's been trying to find places for you all to stay. When you ask for meatballs all the time, I am not sure what to say. And the names you guys call each other, they seem mean. And you guys know I don't work at IKEA. I can't get you a discount."

"Martin, I didn't know you were such a wussy."

"Screw you man," he said, and skated off. A few minutes later, he was back. "Mike, I need to apologize for saying that to you. I didn't mean it."

"So, you're apologizing to me because I called you a wussy? That definitely means you're a wussy."

"Okay, Mike, this is what I mean. So screw you again."

Pat was a blur on the ice. He made the game look easy. He had a hard shot, a nice touch around the net and was the final piece we needed to win. We played for three championships in four seasons, and won two of them in those final years we were together. But Pat wasn't just a flashy skater. The first time he played for us against the dirtiest team with the dirtiest player in the league, I gave him a warning in the pre-game skate to look out for the guy — the first chance they went in the corner, Pat would probably get hit from behind or get a stick in the face.

As fate would have it, on the first trip down the ice, Pat chased a puck into a corner with this guy one step behind. The rest of us cringed, expecting the worst, as Pat seemed oblivious. About two feet from the boards, Pat put on the brakes. His would-be assailant couldn't react in time and crashed into the boards, with the puck between his feet. Pat then lunged, slamming the guy face-first into the boards. The whistle blew. Two minutes for roughing.

He skated by me on his way to the box. I was speechless, waiting to see if the other guy was still alive. Expressionless, Pat said, "That's the guy, right?"

Vlad played the role of the dark Russian for all it was worth. When guys joked about him being former KGB, he never once denied it. He drove a black Mercedes, and when we would ask about his job, he would only say he was in "een-ter-nashional ree-lations." He never smiled, and would hold everyone's attention with stories about being in Moscow when Yeltsin rode the tanks in to escort communism out.

One night, Vlad forgot his water bottles and borrowed one from John. He was grateful, and told John to let him clean the bottle and bring it back refilled the next week. John told him to forget it, but he insisted.

The next week, after a couple of shifts, it seemed John was drinking a lot of water. He called me over.

"Hey man, what does this smell like to you?" he asked.

I took a whiff and it took my breath away. "That's not water, dude."

John looked down the bench at Vlad, who was staring at the action on the ice. "Hey Vlad, did you fill this thing with vodka?"

"No John, only clean it. Vodka make great disinfectant. Is very clean now."

• • •

It seems fitting that a team full of odd characters would find an equally odd sponsor. Sponsoring any sports team — but especially a Beer League team — has to be the worst return on investment a business can make.

But Mikey, a first-generation Italian pizzeria owner, asked no questions. He paid for our uniforms and told us to come by after games, that he would cook us all the pies we wanted. He never let us pay him a dime, even going to so far as to tell us one night we were insulting him.

This comment got the attention of the men we tried to ignore each week, a quartet that sat under a photo of the Rat Pack and spoke in Italian-only every Wednesday night. One had an eye patch. They all looked like extras from "Goodfellas" and had bulges in their jackets. We convinced ourselves that the van always parked across the street was the FBI.

Mikey always had a story, and each week, his whoppers got amped up a notch. We heard about mistresses, fortunes waiting in Italy, shops in New York and how he would soon have pizzerias all over the east coast.

One night stands out. It was early spring, and Mikey saw us coming, so he brought the pizzas out to the patio. "You-ah not-ah going to believe the story I gotta tell," he said, and began talking about his meeting with an "investor."

"So, we at this ah, this ah, nice-a restaurant and he say, Michael, that's a lovely jacket you-ah wearing. I say, ah, thank you, thank-ah you very much. Then he say, Michael, business is good. And I say, yes, business is very good. And he say, I want to invest in you, Michael. And then he say, Michael, let's ah go and let's have the sex now."

All of the side conversations stopped. Mikey took a long drag on his cigarette. We waited to see how he would choose to end this one. Mikey said nothing, he just smoked his cigarette.

"Well?" someone asked.

"Well?" Mikey said. "Well, I gotta de hell outta the restaurant. I was, ah, very upset when I got home. I left my nice jacket at the restaurant. I not gonna go back for the jacket."

• • •

One of my best friends on the team was Reid, a Bostonian. He was so mellow, he always looked high or intoxicated. I once went to an NHL game with him, and he walked all the way through the security entrance, and the ticket scan line drinking a beer. No one said a word to him.

There were two brothers who worked at the rink who bore an uncanny resemblance to the cartoon character Shrek. They were known as Shrek and Shrek Jr. No one in the league could understand a word either of them said. Except for Reid. So, when one of the Shrek brothers would come into the locker room, Reid stood beside him, much like a sign language interpreter, and translate the message —please clean up your towels and empty water bottles — while adding a huge dose of profanity. Neither brother ever figured out what Reid was doing.

In addition to hockey, Reid climbed, kayaked and took part in several Ironman competitions every year. He also smoked. After every game, he could be found enjoying a cigarette in the parking lot with Tommy, one of our best players. Every week, for three years, in an odd ritual, John mooned them both as we got in the car to leave.

· · ·

My hockey stick still fits just right in my hands. Composite shafts, I suppose, are a lot like golf clubs. If a golfer thinks he has an edge with his chosen equipment, then he does. When I knew my playing days were over, I sold my gloves, my shoulder and chest pads and my shin guards. While these items were essential to keeping me alive and able to go to work the mornings after games, I didn't have the sentimental attachment to them like I did my Easton.

I had forgotten the graft job I'd had done at the local hockey shop, even though I could have replaced the entire stick, almost, for what I paid. But it wouldn't have been *that* stick, the one I'd use to score all but a couple of my goals. The black tape and butt end were worn, and there were nicks and cuts and black marks all up and down the shaft. The model name had almost completely been rubbed out. I gripped the stick and got down and set for a wrister right there in the living room, remembering all at once how good the puck feels coming off the blade at the sweet spot, spinning, rising and moving like a fastball. For just a moment, I missed being on the ice, and thought maybe there was some gas left in the tank.

· · ·

If a hockey game is tied after three periods and overtime, a shootout takes place to determine the winner. A puck is placed at center ice, and one player skates out, takes the puck down the ice to go against the goalie, one-on-one. The skater gets one shot. If he scores, his team gets a point. The team with the most points after three shooters wins the game; if the game is tied, it becomes sudden death — a miss coupled with a make ends the game.

A shootout brings out the best or worst in players. Some goalies who were so hard to score on during a game could not handle the pressure of being out there alone. Ditto for skaters.

One season, the league decided to have a shootout after every game, whether there was a tie or not. The winner would get an extra point in the standings. It was great fun, because everyone got a chance to participate in a play that rarely happens in the pros. The Jackals thrived on shootouts. John and I had many shortcomings in the game of hockey. But we had a knack for shootouts.

The highlight of my mostly trivial athletic career came in a shootout. We had been down by one goal in regulation when we pulled Ian to get an extra attacker on with less than 30 seconds left. I went in since I was the freshest skater on the bench at the time. There was a frantic scramble in front of the net, and then the puck squirted loose, floated to my right side and I snapped it high over the glove hand of the keeper and into the net. I looked up. There were three seconds left.

In the shootout, Marc scored, and the other team matched. John skated in and added another, but his counterpart missed. That left me. A make meant a win, and a top four seed in the playoffs. I took the puck at center ice, and slowly plodded towards the goalie. He eased his way out of the net, confident he could cut down my angle as I held the stick and puck out from my body. I got closer, he backed up and covered low, the safe, high percentage play. But as he went down, I snapped my wrists and put the shot exactly where I had sent the game-tying shot. It was beer league hockey, but I had never experienced what it was like to be in the spotlight and take the last shot to win the game. It felt good. It still does.

• • •

Those early years of being horsewhipped made our two championships all the sweeter. The first time we played, we were heavy underdogs to the defending champs, Vinnie's, a team who lost only one game all season, to us, 8-6, on a night when they were only able to field six players. Other than that, the closest anyone had played them was a three-goal loss.

We talked about playing a smart game. We would play tight defense, send all loose pucks out to the wings and up the boards, give up no breakaways and crash the net.

Vinnie's never saw it coming. Three minutes into the game, we were up 3-0. Then, I found myself as the last guy back, with their best player barreling down the ice. I hooked him down with my stick and took the penalty. I sat in the box and knew this would determine the outcome. If they scored on the power play, the entire game could turn around. But Haberkorn scored while we were shorthanded to put us up 4-0. We won 8-2. The Jackals had turned the corner.

The Beer League handed out hideous white caps for winning, but no trophy. We didn't care, we joked about it in Jackals style: we called ourselves Stanley Cap Champions.

The next season, we defended our championship. We had never beaten the team we played in the finals — but we won 7-1. A local sports talk radio station named us Team of the Month and taped a two-minute spot with John, our buddy Adam and me that they ran on a regular loop. We treated it like one of those pro wrestling interviews. Every time the DJ called us league champions, we corrected him by saying "two-time champions." We pointed out that we rarely practiced and never talked strategy.

• • •

In a frame in our hallway at home are two team photographs taken just minutes after we won those championships. We did a team pose just like the NHL Stanley Cup winners do — the goalie stretched across the foreground and the team ganged around. Each of us is smiling ear-to-ear. Most everyone has their arms around the players on either side. There is an electricity to the photo, an elation that you can sense. It is obvious that we were all friends. I find myself mirroring those smiles every time I look at those photos. I miss those guys. I know we'll never get together again.

When the shutter opened and closed on those images, I couldn't imagine a time in the future without hockey. When life or your body demands that you stop doing something that you used to do with ease, you come to understand how so many ex-professional athletes have troubled or unhappy lives after they give up the game.

John is still my best friend. We don't get together quite as much since my kids are all into their own activities and sports, and he coaches high school sports and is about to get married. Hockey gave us an excuse to hang out and do something. Reid calls every once in a while. I talk and text with Adam, and see Martin, Trae, Testa, Tommy, Ian and Paul on Facebook. J.B. is back in Europe and Pat went back to Canada. I lost track of Jonah, Vlad, Creed, Manaro and Hodges. Marc got his MBA and his pilot's license and when I saw a TV news report about a single engine plane landing and flipping on I-40, I just knew it was him. It wasn't.

I miss the biting cold of the rink, lacing my skates so tight I can feel the blood pumping and taking that first warm-up lap around the ice. I miss snapping those wrist shots past the goalie, hanging around the net to stuff home a garbage goal, or making a pass to a teammate who scores. I miss the hits, and I even miss being hit, being reminded of being part of something. Mostly, I miss my unlikely collection of friends, guys I would have never met or had a word with if not for the forced circumstances of Beer League hockey. I miss knowing that no matter what was going on in the world, someone would say the most stupid thing at just the wrong time to make the day better.

• • •

13

Promises

We stood on the concrete steps of the weathered, green stucco dorm. It was early October, but the brisk wind made it seem more like late November. She was talking nervously, rambling. Filling the space between us. There was a little tremble in her voice. She rubbed her arms to warm herself, and I watched and listened and said nothing. When she paused for just a second, I leaned in and kissed her.

I am not sure who was the most surprised. My inexperience in such matters surely added to the clumsiness. The kiss lingered in the sound of passing cars. People coming and going from the dorm disappeared, and a warmth wrapped around me. A whiff of perfume drifted by, and then it was over. Neither of us said anything, but somewhere in there had to be a "good night" or "see you tomorrow."

As I got into my Chevette, I took a deep breath before starting the engine. I thought to myself that I was going to marry that girl.

• • •

It doesn't happen every day. Not anymore. But sometimes, I do think about our two babies who died.

More often, I think more about the time the doctors thought our daughter might have a brain tumor, or the time they thought our oldest son might no longer be alive on the day he was born. Or the time our youngest son had to have surgery.

But, inevitably, my wife or I will see someone we haven't seen in years, or meet someone new. When that person asks the ages of our children, there is almost always a remark about the age gap between the oldest two. I guess most folks think that in a time of planning life like a business, there is no explanation for such a pause.

• • •

The first time I saw her was in my freshman history class at Barton College, "Western Civ to 1789." It was a small class, and I sat in back with a buddy from high school. She sat upfront, a strawberry blonde, with big hazel eyes. She was smart, loved history and was easy on the eyes.

I'd had little prior success with girls, short of one two-month fling the summer after my senior year of high school. I never went to the prom. I had crushes, but they never amounted to anything.

Despite my best efforts, I couldn't cross paths with the girl from history class. That is, until the signups started for intramural sports. My buddy and I showed up at the field a couple of blocks from campus and waited for the student worker to show up. Only two other students came, and then the student worker arrived — it was the strawberry blonde.

Due to lack of turnout, we went over to the gym. We played ping pong for a while, and as we were getting ready to go, she came by to check on us. I couldn't remember her name — our history professor called roll by last name only. Had she told us at the field? I was embarrassed and had no line, so I finally asked: "What did you say your name was?"

Without missing a beat, she turned her mouth in an innocent, mock surprised way, lifted her hand and spun her class ring around. "It's Kristi," she said, "yeah, that's what it says right here." She walked away, smiling, and said she'd see us in class.

"Dude, you have got to ask that girl out," my buddy said.

• • •

We had been married for seven years when Kristi and I thought maybe it was time to start a family. After a year, we realized it wasn't going to be as easy as people made it out to be. Another year of fertility drugs, tests, charts, tracking, testing and timing made me realize I should have paid more attention in math and biology class. We were informed that conception might not be possible. Then finally, one day, Kristi got two pink lines instead of the usual one. She went through a box of tests before visiting the doctor who quickly confirmed she was pregnant.

Holly was born in the spring of 2000, and came into the world amidst a crowd of two families waiting for the first grandchild on either side in ten years. The nurse handed me the most beautiful, bald, little girl I'd ever seen. I never wanted to put her down. For weeks, I would hold Holly until she fell asleep, and then I'd lay her on the couch beside me and watch her and wonder how incomplete my life had been until that moment.

At Holly's six-month checkup, the pediatrician seemed uncomfortable. He recommended a trip to the university hospital in Greenville, since something didn't seem right with Holly's eyes. We had noticed we could not get her attention at times. The doctor was evasive, until I finally pressed so hard, he mentioned, "tumor."

The specialist set up tests, including a CAT scan. I stood in the dark room, took off my watch and my wedding band, and slid on a lead apron. I held five tiny fingers in my hand as the table rotated. Holly was still and silent, just staring at me with those big brown eyes, with less fear than I had. I promised her in that moment before the radiation came into the room, that I would never let go.

• • •

I started showing up for class early, just to get a chance to talk to Kristi. It took some time to build the nerve up to ask her out. On our first date, we went to an on-campus a production of "The Bad Seed." There was chemistry right from the start, and we talked for hours after the performance. She was from an idyllic town near the Shenandoah Valley, had played varsity basketball and was homecoming queen her senior year. Things got hot and heavy and after just a weeks, it was like we had been together for years.

• • •

Holly's tests and scans and exams came back. It wasn't a brain tumor, it was an eye development issue. She wears glasses now. After spending time in children's hospital wards, we realized how small our problems and worries had been.

• • •

The first time we lost a child, it was very clinical. A routine checkup showed some skewed numbers, other signs followed, and then it was over. We had just told everyone that Kristi was pregnant.

Well-wishers said, "You can always try again." Doctors said, "It just happens sometimes." Ministers said, "God knows what he's doing, trust him." None of that helped at the moment of grief. Kristi took it hard, blamed herself, and tried to figure out what she had done. I was helpless, hurting, and all I could do was put my arms around her.

• • •

Kristi and I talked on the phone every night while she was home in the Virginia mountains during Christmas break. The separation was awful. Three weeks after she got back to school, we broke up. She started dating her jogging partner, a mutual friend. I hated that guy. I still do.

• • •

The next time it happened, I was jolted from a deep sleep in the middle of the night by a voice crying for help. It was Kristi, and I found her in the bathroom, holding onto the wall with one arm and clutching her abdomen with the other. She was crying and telling me we had to get to the hospital. I got her to the edge of the bed and could tell the cramping was getting worse. Both of us knew what was happening.

I called my mom, who lived next door, and asked if she could come stay with Holly. She was at the door in minutes and we were out, speeding towards the hospital in Rocky Mount, thirty minutes away. Within an hour, our doctor had to tell us that our baby had died. We had seen, and heard the heartbeat just a few days before.

We felt a collective weight, a darkness descend that we could not see lifted. We thanked God for Holly, and we accepted that she might be our only child. This was more than many people were allowed to ever have.

• • •

Despite being on a small campus, Kristi and I went two years largely avoiding each other and rarely speaking. It was weird. We avoided being in the same room whenever possible, until we ended up in another history class our junior year. There was one seat left when I got to class on the first day; it was next to her.

Pretty soon, if one of us missed class, the other shared lecture notes. Sometimes we ate lunch together. The idea of being friends was on the table, but we each vowed repeatedly there would be no advancement of the relationship.

A guest speaker was scheduled for our class one night, a well-known Marxist conspiracy theorist who had made his name in the 1960s, and almost 30 years later was still riding the coattails of his battle against The Man. We decided to walk to the lecture together.

Two hours later, when the presentation finally ended and our professor seemed on the verge of an academically-induced climax, we walked back debating who was crazier, the speaker or the folks who paid him to make appearances. We got in the elevator, I pushed the button for her floor, and when I turned around, Kristi stepped up on her tiptoes and kissed me.

• • •

When the doctor injects your wife in the arm with a "fertility cocktail," then turns around, pats you on the back, and says, "Good luck," what else is there to do besides giggle like a middle schooler? As we left the university's women's clinic, all the nurses and staff we'd come to know over the previous months passed us in the hallway, and with devilish grins, offered encouragements.

This time, the pregnancy went well. Kristi's doctor suggested inducing labor as he projected a large baby. The date was set and we arrived at the hospital hopeful. We checked in, IVs were started, sensors clipped, drugs administered and everything was on go. Kristi was resting, machines were beep-beep-beeping her vitals and the baby's. I took a seat near the bed and tried to read *Band of Brothers*, but couldn't concentrate. It was quiet, so I flipped on the Red Sox-Yankees game. It was Opening Day 2005. I thought that was a good sign.

But then Kristi's breathing changed, as did her heart rate. She was disoriented. Before I could call for a nurse, one appeared, followed shortly by a doctor. There was poking and prodding and I was nudged away from the bedside as more staff showed up. They had lost the heartbeat of the baby — a boy, ultrasounds indicated — and I heard someone say "we need to stabilize her." Everything in the room started moving, and I could feel the churn in my stomach. I heard "she seems okay for now." As I steadied myself by gripping the back of the chair, the doctor assured me he'd be right back. The monitor for the baby was silent. Soon, the doctor was back, and they searched for a heartbeat that could not be found. He told me that it happened sometimes, it wasn't necessarily bad, that the baby could have turned or shifted, or was ready … and that the operating room was being prepped for a C-section if needed. I wanted to ask questions, but he was gone before I could decide what to ask.

Then they were right back. The doctor pulled me away from the hospital bed and told me that I might have to make some tough decisions, and make them quickly. I didn't know what that meant. There was still no heartbeat. It could be nothing, or it could be a tangled umbilical cord, he said, and headed out the door.

Then the doctor was back. Things are starting to happen he said.

"Okay."

"Let's have a baby," he said.

I reached for the TV, to turn the game off.

"Leave it on," the doctor said, "that might be cool."

I noticed nurses were in place.

"Who ya pulling for," he asked.

"Red Sox."

"Here we go. I see a baby."

Kristi gasped. The drugs were wearing off.

"What's the score?"

I was white knuckling the bed rail. I saw arms, legs, a head, a torso. All blue.

No sound.

There was a huddle. Our baby was on a table.

No sound.

No sight.

Suddenly, a nurse handed me a white bundle, topped with a blue and white cap. I realized I was holding my breath. "Want to hold your son, Mr. Brantley?"

I looked down and was met by two beady, questioning eyes and a wrinkled brow. It was like the boy wanted to ask me a question. I pulled him near me, he was warm, soft, clean, beautiful. He was Junior, to be called Kent.

She should hold him first, I told the nurse, nodding at Kristi, she did all the work.

• • •

I proposed to Kristi over Christmas Break our senior year. There would be no taking chances this time around.

• • •

"Dr. B wants to check me for cancer."

I didn't quite say it that way, but it was pretty close. Despite fluctuating weight issues, I've always been an active and healthy guy. At 37, I wasn't on any prescriptions, I'd never had an IV, and had never been admitted to a hospital, not even for an outpatient procedure.

No one really wants to know the details of a colonoscopy. Let's just say there are less humiliating ways to spend a day. Kristi and I didn't talk about it much, other than to say a prayer. While I didn't feel invincible like I did at 18, I had not really considered the possibility of a problem. I had a wife, a six-year-old and a one-year-old, as well as a successful business. When the nurse prepped me, and rolled me on a gurney to a room of people waiting for the same procedure, I wondered who among us would be getting bad news that day. The nurse said I looked flush, and that maybe she should get my wife before I went in because I was sweating a lot. I told her this was new stuff for me, needles and anesthesia.

"Well, then, you are a blessed man, sir. A blessed man for sure."

I was thinking about those words when they gave me the first set of tranquilizers. They asked me to count backwards from 100, and when I got to 70, I told them maybe they should hit me again. I didn't count anymore. I wanted a promise, or promises, that I would see my babies grow up, and the chance to grow old with the love of my life. And then everything disappeared.

. . .

My dreams play in my head like movies. There are close-ups and wide shots and the cinematography is excellent. I sometimes dream about all of the battlefields I've walked with my wife, the colors, the time of year subtle in the distance. Our modest honeymoon to Edenton, a 300-year-old town on the Albemarle Sound in North Carolina, steeped in history, plays well. It is autumn, and trees that stood since before the Revolution yield their leaves in the background as we walk the sidewalks, the square, the waterfront, and visit the old Courthouse. We take turns on the bench. The bed and breakfast where we stay in is an old plantation house, with tall windows, and the room has a canopy bed. Our trips to hockey games, feature rich red and black contrasts, as we cheer our Hurricanes to two Stanley Cup finals. The libraries where we spend time reading or researching together are peaceful, quiet, and always offer a seating area with a view of the outside world, out of focus, but there. I dreamed all of those things the day I found out I didn't have cancer.

. . .

I must have gotten my money's worth on the painkillers. When I woke up, Kristi was smiling and the doctor said, "Good news." An orderly wheeled me to the car and helped me get in. I'm not sure how I got home and into my own bed.

"Hey, I need to tell you something and then I'll leave you alone," Kristi said. "I'm pregnant."

I would have thought I dreamed the whole thing had Kristi not lined the bathroom counter and the bathtub with positive home pregnancy tests. She is thorough that way.

We were in unchartered territory those nine months. This was the first pregnancy with no fertility help. The risk, while not spoken of, certainly hung in the air, but the irony of finding out about a new life, a new beginning, on a day that could have been about an ending, clearly seemed to be a Divine sign.

Kristi's doctors wanted to leave nothing to chance. We'd be referred to another university hospital, this time in Raleigh, for tests and screenings and all the trappings of an "at risk" pregnancy. We would also get "counseling" before each procedure, according to the paperwork.

We were led to an office where several scenarios were laid out before us. We were told that there were many tests available and we should make use of them. At our "advanced ages," there was a good chance for all kinds of issues the brusque counselor told us. For example, our baby might have Down's or any number of imperfections, and technology would let us know so we could make appropriate choices. I felt the heat of the words singe my face. I glanced at Kristi. She looked horrified, as we both knew what choices meant.

"You can stop right there," I said.

"It is hospital policy—"

"I'll sign whatever paper you need signed that says we had this talk and passed. But we need to be done on this." I felt Kristi squeeze my hand. This woman was doing her job, but I was doing mine. Protecting. She didn't realize what we had been through, that there was still an emptiness for us.

Kristi had tears in her eyes. "This is not a thing, it is our baby. You don't have a test that can change that," I said.

There was an awkward silence. Maybe later, I was the subject at a water cooler or at dinner or in a lounge, portrayed as some wild-eyed religious zealot, or as a bully who imposes his will on his wife. I'm okay with being judged by people who think they aren't judgmental.

• • •

Kristi gave birth to another son, our third child, a few months after that meeting. While she was sick for the entire pregnancy, it was her easiest delivery. The doctor almost missed the show, and the epidural was so effective, Kristi suggested we go ahead and have another while we were there.

Later when Lowell was three, he had to have his tonsils and adenoids removed. Three severe breathing attacks and trips to the emergency room in six months had left us little choice. The most difficult moment of my life was when they came to take him away to the operating room. He made us promise to be there when he got back. We did. He climbed into a little red Radio Flyer wagon, and a nurse pulled him down one corridor, and pretended she had accidentally gone the wrong way, so he could make one last lap. He grinned and waved and called to us as they wheeled him around the corner.

We hoped he didn't see the worry on our faces, or the tears that formed. The hour in that nice, comfortable waiting room was awful. The doctor had told us 45 minutes and we'd be called back. Had something gone wrong? Kristi was worried Lowell would wake up and we wouldn't be there. He did, and was terrified, unable to cry out in a room full of strangers. It turned out the nurse who was supposed to come get us had taken a phone call on the way out, an innocent enough break for her, but a gut-wrenching one for us.

We got to the recovery room and saw Lowell. He had dark circles around his eyes, and there was fear as well as relief in his body language. He wrapped his arms around us in the warmest, strongest, but most fragile embrace I've ever felt. We held him until he stopped crying.

• • •

About six months after Lowell's surgery, a respected photographer colleague and friend created a family portrait for us. A large print hangs on our living room wall, just above the sofa. It is just one-sixtieth of a second in the life of our family.

We're all wearing dark shirts and blue jeans. Kristi and I are seated, as close as we can possibly get to each other. Holly has her arms locked in mine, and Kent is holding onto Kristi, with his head on her shoulder. Lowell shares our laps, right in the middle of the frame. It is well done, but more importantly, we look happy, all of us, regardless of whatever trials and spats and stresses and concerns came before that shutter opened and what has followed since it closed once again.

• • •

14

The Real Thing

As soon as he saw me, he said, "Michael! I hope you ain't forgot all the things I taught you." He was older now, retired, but he still had that mischievous lilt in his voice.

I hadn't seen Larry[1] in almost 15 years, but I did remember most of the things he taught me in my last summer job before I joined the real world. I shook his hand warmly, took a pat on the back and invited him into my camera room.

"Maybe you can teach me some more stuff," I said.

He smiled. "Always, son, always!"

• • •

I stood, frozen, on one side of the counter. A very muscular and menacing-looking, tattooed Hispanic man stood on the other, the very portrait of a TV crime drama gang-banger. In a quick, fluid motion, he pulled a switchblade out of his pants pocket and pointed it towards me.

---

[1] Larry was his real name, and he was larger than life.

"You can use this," he said.

Without taking my eyes off the blade, I mumbled something about how I was going back outside to check the truck again. I stepped quickly out of the store and into the parking lot, as the clerk called after me to come back in if I wanted to use his knife.

I'd been sent across the wrong side of the tracks, close to quitting time on a Friday afternoon, under the dark skies of a looming eastern North Carolina thunderstorm[2] — the kind that is particularly nasty in August. I was tasked with hanging a banner on the convenience store's sign by the road, hawking 99-cent two liter Coca-Colas.

I had forgotten to grab a toolbox on my way out of the plant's parking lot in downtown Rocky Mount, and the old banner had to be cut down before the new one could go up. I asked the clerk for a pair of scissors and had been offered a weapon of dubious provenance.

With lightning streaking across the sky, I used the truck bed for a ladder. The white and red banner came down and the new one went up. I climbed down from the truck and into the cab, cranked the engine, and lowered the window just enough to keep some air circulating as I headed back over the tracks. I had just completed another week at the most physically demanding, highest paying job I'd ever had, working for the local Coca-Cola distributor.

• • •

Just before my senior year at Barton College in Wilson, my best friend and I decided we wanted to move into an apartment. For me, this meant I needed to earn and save. I had plenty of time, as my girlfriend, Kristi, was spending the summer working in Alaska. A cousin who managed a large independent grocery store knew the Coke plant manager, who needed some summer help. I was told to shave, put on a coat and tie and

---

[2] There are two types of weather in NC in the summer: 95 degrees or driving rainstorms. Sometimes, you get both simultaneously.

report to the plant to apply for a job as a "swing man,"[3] a nice title that simply meant the college kid who did the jobs no one else wanted to do.

I like to think I made a good impression with my smarts and manner, but in reality it was most likely the fact that farm work and sports had made me into a 6-foot-2, 225-pound fullback. I was hired on the spot, issued a Coke truckers hat, a red Coca-Cola t-shirt, two white-and-green pinstripe, button-down shirts and two pairs of green pants. I was told — with a smile — to be at the plant at 7:30 am on Monday.

It was the Coca-Cola way of doing business — everyone was expected to be professional — from the drivers, to the front office dispatchers and bookkeepers to the guys unloading 18-wheelers by hand and by forklift. Coke guys knew they were the real thing, and that came with a little swagger.

On my first day, I was assigned to ride with Bart[4], a by-the-book type with black bushy hair, and a matching '80s mustache. He was slouchy, and constantly hitched up his pants while urging people to work harder and complaining that they didn't. Bart was a supervisor, and he gave me an orientation as we rode 20 minutes down U.S. 301 South to Wilson to fill up a delivery truck at a small warehouse.

Bart painted a grim picture. Summer workers were usually slack, he said. All workers were to go as hard as they could from the moment of clock-in, they should try to make up the time spent on break, try not to take a lunch hour, and occupy all free time by doing odd jobs around the plant. I listened and didn't say much as we bounced along the highway, confident that my last summer break was slowly swirling down the toilet.

By the time we got back to Rocky Mount, dread had settled in. I would have to prove myself to the blue collar crew. I didn't curse, and I was already sweating, so it was obvious I must not be used to hard work. The only thing in my favor was my car, a Camaro RS I'd saved for four

---

[3] It still beat shoveling hog manure. By a mile.
[4] Bart is not his real name. He was kind of like Barney Fife without the humor or likeability.

years to buy. These guys were car guys, NASCAR fans, and Tom Cruise's new movie, "Days of Thunder," was hot stuff. My car knowledge was limited to two things: 1) My Camaro was a five-speed V8, and 2) It could go really, really fast.

That afternoon, I went out to help a driver named Carl[5]. Carl gave me a different perspective on my job. Bart, as he put it, was "Full of shit because he makes everybody work and he usually just ends up watching;" college boys had a bad name because "Harold[6], has been at the community college for about five years, and ain't worth a damn;" and "Coca-Cola is a good place to work."

My job shaped up pretty quickly. Each day, I was assigned to a driver who was expected to have the hardest day. I provided extra muscle. Sometimes I'd ride shotgun with the driver, other times I'd take a pickup truck with a radio, call in when the driver released me and head to the next stop.

For my trouble, I would be paid $5.79 an hour, about 25 percent over minimum wage at the time, and then time-and-a-half for overtime. I would have to work every other Saturday pulling stock on a route. I could have had part of my pay deducted to buy Coke stock at a discount — a benefit I was not mature enough to take advantage of[7]. I still regret that.

• • •

Rocky Mount, North Carolina, population 58,000, was once the national headquarters for the Hardee's restaurant chain and two 100-year-old banks. It was home to one of the top two tobacco markets in the world, had several textile mills and was an active freight market with a postcard Old South downtown.

---

[5] Carl is not his real name. But I think his mama would be upset if she knew he cussed.
[6] It's true. Harold wasn't worth a damn. He probably married money.
[7] That stock today would be worth a lot more money than I made that summer.

It is a city that straddles two counties, Nash and Edgecombe, and is divided, literally, by two sets of north-south railroad tracks. All of the major businesses, commerce and valuable real estate were on the Nash or "right side" of the tracks, while the Edgecombe side was home to most of the crime, poverty and unemployed. It was the "wrong side" of the tracks, home to a growing drug trade and the emergence of a gang culture that has grown exponentially.

The banks merged and have been bought up and moved out of town. Hardee's is gone, and the mills, too. There has been flight from the city limits in all areas and jobs are hard to come by. The mall that was once the biggest and best east of Raleigh — named after the city's tobacco heritage — has lost some of its biggest stores and had a series of shootings.

• • •

Youthful naivety told me I was smarter than anyone else at Coca-Cola. After all, I was practically a college graduate. I soon learned there are different types of smart. A smart driver was a steady worker, who was gracious to store managers, and held doors for customers.

I was amazed at how many flats of 12-ounce cans the veterans could stack and roll into a store on their heavy duty hand trucks. It was nothing to see them rolling nearly 400 cans in a trip or never missing a beat with 60 or more two-liters, leaving just enough room to see around the hand truck. This was heavy, awkward weight and took some agility to maneuver, something you can't appreciate — and would never even think about — until you've tried, and failed at it. After a series of near disasters with doorjambs, uneven floors and unattended children, I resigned myself to carrying loads of about 75 percent of what the drivers did.

The guys at least appreciated my intentions. Most of them would give me six packs of drinks off their trucks and buy me lunch. I tried to beg off their kindness at first, until one, Tim[8], laid it out for me one day. "Look man, when you help me, my day ends at three instead of seven. I got time to go home, cut my grass, and chill out before my wife gets off from work. I can work on my racecar. A hamburger and fries is a bargain. Most summer help won't work hard, they know they're leaving in August."

Tim's words and easy going nature made him my favorite driver to ride with. His attitude and work ethic had surely played a role in getting a good, profitable route. The drivers with the best routes — which meant the busiest stores — could not keep shelves stocked in the summer, especially when two-liters went on sale for 89 cents or sometimes even 69 cents. Soft drinks were big in the early 1990s. The only sports drink was Gatorade, and most folks still mixed their own. Sugary drinks were not an item under attack by the government and media, they were cheap and they flew off the shelves, especially in the ridiculously hot and humid summers.

Drivers had pressure on them. In addition to working hard, there was a code of conduct, both professional and practical. Any traffic violations from speeding to DWI, whether on the job or off, was grounds for immediate dismissal. Insurance costs had to be contained. Dismissal of an employee was sobering because the Coke crew was a tight one, but it also meant that everyone below the man who got the axe moved up — better routes were earned through retirements, promotions of veterans to supervisors or firings. In a way, it was kind of the like the funeral of an uncle you might not be close to; everyone mourned for a few days, and then awaited the reading of the will.

• • •

The Eckerd Drug Store chain is extinct now, but for years after working

---

[8] Tim reminded me a lot of my brother, but never hung me upside down from the ceiling.

at Coke, I could not ride past one without smiling and remembering the day I almost triggered a 911 call at the delivery entrance on the wrong side of the tracks.

I reached for the top rack on the side of the truck and grabbed a crate of two liter Diet Cokes. When I did, the plastic crate split, and the drinks rained down from nearly eight feet high. One just barely missed my head, and struck the ground hard, cap down. A pop followed and the drink tumbled over and took off like a torpedo, nailing the back door of the drugstore with an echoing thud, followed by two more in almost the exact spot. Tim rolled in laughter and I could only stand and watch. Just as the last drink whizzed by the door and out of sight, a thin, weasel-looking manager stuck his head out. His look of fear quickly turned to anger, and he yelled, "What the hell are you doing out here?" I looked to where Tim had just been standing. He was gone, off in a flash around to the other side of the truck, snickering just loud enough for me to hear him, urging me to make something up. "I banged the door when I dropped my hand truck," I managed to say, trying to hold in my laughter and ignore Tim, who was now criticizing my lack of creativity. Oblivious to the carbonation all over the asphalt, the manager yelled again, "You scared the hell out of us. Don't make me call your boss." He slammed the door, allowing me to notice the imprint of bottle caps in the lower portion of the steel door.

Tim came back around, slapping his thigh while I tried to take it all in. "Oh yeah, man, by the way," he said "it's cool as hell when a two liter hits the pavement cap down."

• • •

Most people probably don't think of soft drink delivery as a multicultural experience. It made my world on the farm seem even smaller. I saw kindness, poverty, excess, dishonesty, and brutality. In the morning, we might be in high-end stores, full of young suburban women, then off to a country club poolside vending machine, then to a Middle Eastern market before ending the day at a soul food butcher.

At one Middle Eastern market, the proprietor spoke broken English, mostly comprised of profanity. He always complained that we shorted him on his order, despite the fact that we'd count it twice for him and allow him to count it; he would wait until we started stocking his cooler to say we'd held back a crate — a point no one could prove. The drivers always held their ground. Coke didn't make billions in profit by getting snookered. I watched the guy one day and realized that he was accepting Toys R Us dollars as payment for 25 cents on the dollar, and that he would let customers buy cigarettes and malt liquor with food stamps, again for a leveraged exchange rate. He would brag to us about how much money he made that way, and how easy it was.

In those days, soft drinks were on a complex pricing schedule. For example, if a store wanted to run a special on two-liter drinks at 69 cents, the price would be set below that. Proprietors and managers were expected to put the sale price on for the entire agreed upon promotion time; violation would result in being billed for full price that week. Drivers sometimes caught vendors changing their signs as soon as the truck was out of sight. This often required no more than circling the block and coming back with a threat of ending delivery service.

There were other examples of gaming the system. The most common trick involved the fountain drink dispensers at convenience stores. Coca-Cola has a very precise mix of syrup and CO_2 that combines to make each drink taste just perfect. Syrup was expensive; CO_2 was not. The guys who delivered the "bag-in-a-box" syrup and set up the machines could nail that formula in a matter of minutes, creating drinks that balanced quality with profit. Disreputable managers found that by dialing down the syrup and dialing up the carbonation, they could squeeze several more flat-tasting drinks out of a box of syrup, which over the course of a year added up to serious money. This type of cheating was easily detected because it often caused problems with the fountain units.

While most drivers were likeable, not all were endearing. T-Bone[9] was a prime example. He didn't have a good route, and he'd always talk about how he was going to get someone else's. He always said it in a joking way, and no one considered him a threat, because he was lazy. But he loved to joke, and he looked a lot like the comedian Cedric the Entertainer.

In the first half of the century, Coca-Cola offered home delivery in town to anyone who wanted it, and there was no minimum order. The practice had long been discontinued, but a few little old ladies were grandfathered in. T-Bone had to service all of these accounts, which numbered about half a dozen. One day we pulled up on the steep hill in front of the first house, and he stopped on the street.

Since I rode in all the trucks, I knew them as well as anyone. The lower-rung drivers didn't always get the same truck. "You think it's a good idea to stop on this hill?" I asked. We had one of the older trucks, a stick shift, with a giant hand brake in the floor, which tended to slip.

"C'mon man! I'm been driving this truck since you was in third grade or something. You just get them drinks out of the back. You can get them all, wanting to know if I can park this truck. Man!" he said, feigning insult. I put a crate of glass bottle Cokes on the hand truck and pushed it to the curb. When I looked back, the truck was easing down the hill.

"T-Bone!"

"Hush up now, I got to deal with the customer!" he yelled at me, without even looking.

"Alright then, but there goes your truck!"

T-Bone looked back. "Oh, damn! You got to catch my truck man, go! C'mon man, run!"

The neighborhood was quiet, and the streets were empty. A mean streak in me kicked in, so I just jogged after the truck, knowing who would be responsible — not the college boy.

"C'mon, Mike! I know you white, but you faster than that. C'mon,

---

[9] No one was mad years later when T-Bone got fired. I gave him a better alias than he deserved.

man!" I waited for T-Bone to catch up and then took off after the passenger side while he waddled after the driver's side. Still at the age of feeling invincible, I foolishly jumped on the running board, opened the truck door, lunged across the seat and yanked at the hand brake, jerking the old wagon to a halt. T-Bone jumped in and grabbed the wheel. "Damn, I'm glad I caught this truck." He looked at me and didn't like what he saw. "New, I mean, you did good Mike, you alright. Hey look, you can't tell nobody at the plant, you can't say nothing."

"This is too good to let go, T-Bone."

"Look now, Mike, I'll leave your ass if I have to. You got to promise me you won't say a word." I agreed, certain that he would leave me. When we got back to the plant, he put me out and headed for lunch. When he came back, the warehouse was deserted. All the guys were in the break room, looking at my drawing on the chalkboard of a round figure chasing a truck down a hill while a stick man waved from the running board. I was sitting at the table, not saying a word; while the drivers had the most fun they'd had all week. I never rode with T-Bone again, but all the drivers made a point of telling me how smart I was the rest of the summer.

• • •

A few years ago, I was saddened to see the obituary for Larry, one of the service guys from Coca-Cola. I didn't get to ride with those guys much. They were a different breed from the rest of the Coke team. The service guys were all nearing retirement, and no one was being trained to replace them. The service guys thought of themselves as the Special Forces of Coca-Cola. They worked on machines that dated back to the 1940s, all the way up to the latest digital ones. And they kept them all running. The hung out together, took long lunches, worked at their own pace and had authority to do whatever was needed.

Larry was a character. He was a Vietnam Vet, and he talked about his time in service. He loved the Army, and had stayed in the National Guard when the war was over. He was upset he missed out on Grenada, but always claimed to be ready to go whenever Uncle Sam called. I heard he volunteered and went to the Persian Gulf War in 1991, and came back mad that the Army didn't finish the job.

Larry told me that the military had taught him how to live his life and he was going to pass it on to me, "free of charge." We took the long ride to service jobs, never going over the speed limit and we never went back in without getting ice cream, because Larry said, "ice cream is good, and I like it."[10] Larry always bought and told me that one day I would be the guy who bought a kid ice cream.

My favorite thing about Larry was his military-related paranoia. He had plenty of wisdom: always size up everyone when you walk into a store, and know who the threats are; never trust anybody; never be more than arm's length from something you can kill somebody with; when you find a good woman, lock her down before someone else does; and always look under your car for booby traps. But Larry's best habit was "never go back the way you came, someone might be waiting for you." He said that philosophy kept him alive in Vietnam and worked just fine in Rocky Mount, too. And he stuck by it. We never, ever, drove back to the plant on the same route, and if he had days where he'd let me drive so he could catch a nap, he'd insist that he'd checked the odometer before giving me the wheel and he'd know if I didn't follow his orders. [11]

I was able to do nice portraits for him and his wife when they came in to celebrate their 50th Wedding Anniversary. His wife had made the appointment, and the last name didn't register with me. If I had known he was coming, I would have had ice cream in the freezer. That day, I took a different route home from work, just to be safe.

---

[10] This was my favorite Larry-ism.
[11] Larry and I never did get ambushed.

• • •

I cannot walk down the soft drink aisle of a grocery store without taking note of how the shelf is stocked. Whenever I see empty gaps where Sprites or Diet Coke should be, especially if it is a weekend, I can't help but think the Coca-Cola guys would not be happy.

A key part of my job that summer was to pull stock. This meant taking a Coke pickup truck on a Saturday route to make sure all the big grocery stores had the shelves full of product for thirsty shoppers.

It was lonely duty. By the time I finished work, my friends were already out — it was after all, the last summer of fun. I daydreamed while puttering around in the truck and counting stock. The work in front of me, replacing drinks for the weekend, seemed simple and satisfying. What I would do after graduation seemed less clear.

The big retailers, like K-Mart, Wal-Mart, and other megastores required more drastic measures, especially on sale weekends. Drivers would fill the allotted area in the back of the store, go back to the plant, refill the truck with a maximum load and then leave the truck in the store's parking lot. On more than one occasion, drivers would have to refill the truck again before the weekend was over. It gave a real life picture of "scale" I heard during boring lectures in Macroeconomics. If a city the size of Rocky Mount had such an insatiable appetite for Dr. Pepper and Mello Yello that a fully mobilized plant could not satisfy the needs for one weekend, how many drinks was Coca-Cola selling across the world in a day?

One Friday, as the summer was winding down and I was feeling confident that I had mastered this summer job, I got what I thought was light duty. I was told to go to the local Farm Fresh grocery store, and spend the day making sure the display stayed stocked. A truck was already there, full, and the route driver had built the display. At a price of 69 cents for a two-liter, though, the display would probably need some work by the time I got there.

I loaded a hand truck and rolled it in when I arrived. The display was already missing about a quarter of the stock. I rolled in more drinks, only to find the display was down to half. I was losing ground. I set in to my work as the store got busier with morning shoppers. As midday neared, customers started grabbing drinks off my hand truck.

Apparently the manager of the store saw me struggling and called for backup. A couple of guys from the plant showed up and joined in the battle. We emptied the truck and another one was called in, and I had yet to top off the display. More Coke employees showed up. I bumped into someone as I worked frantically, looked up, and saw the plant manager next to me, in his tie, slinging drinks just as hard as the rest of us. At three o'clock, when I finally got the display full, I realized all of the non-route workers and all of the supervisors were standing around, stacking drinks. I looked at the plant manager and he just grinned at me.

Those guys were a team, doing their jobs well and taking home a nice paycheck. Summer help came and went in 90 days, but these men stood shoulder-to-shoulder for decades, getting their hands dirty.

When I left Coca-Cola to go back to college, I had money in the bank to pay my rent for the school year. I had toned up and gotten stronger, and was a little less dumb that I had been in June. My situation had been temporary, and I was glad that I wouldn't spend a lifetime working that hard. Maybe, too, I'd learned a lesson about judging people and their jobs. For sure, I didn't leave by the same route I came.

• • •

15

Me and John and Gus and Hairy

I could not see anyone — not the other pallbearers, not even the person next to me. Later, I heard the place was packed, but I could have sworn I was in there by myself. My eyes burned with salt from the sweat and the tears and I thought to myself, "Get some control, man." I was doing something I'd never done in public before: weeping uncontrollably and sniffling for breath.

Just a few feet away, in a beautiful, awful, brushed nickel casket, lay my brother-in-law, John. I wanted to get up, to stop the nonsense, to go down the road to his house and shoot one more game of pool and talk about UNC basketball, to go outside at Mama's house for one last game of one-on-one.

I felt a tap on my left knee.

"It's time to go," a voice said.

• • •

I was five when my oldest sister Carol said she was bringing her new boyfriend over to meet our parents. He had been mentioned around the house a lot, but I was pretty sure I was not going to like this guy. Carol was like a second mama to me, fussing over me and spoiling me — and I did not need any competition for her time. Whoever this boyfriend "John" was, he had to go.

It was a Friday night. I was deep into a strategic placement of my hand-me-down G.I. Joes when Carol walked into the house with a stereotype of the 1970s. My parents' first impression of the tall, goofy guy with the big black hair, black-rimmed, photo-gray glasses, bushy beard and Magnum, P.I. mustache must have been shock. To top it all off, he smelled like Christmas. I just stared at him as introductions were made, and waited for my turn. He beat me to the punch.

"Well, well," he said loudly, "you must be Gus. I've heard all about you. What's happening, Gus?"

My face and ears burned. I looked at my mama and she looked bewildered. "I ain't Gus," I said, "I'm Michael."

Without missing a beat, the man said, "Hmph. You look like a Gus to me. I think I'll just call you that." And then he laughed, only he sounded like the Saturday morning cartoon dog, Muttley. There was some sort of asthmatic wheeze, followed by a body tremble before he started laughing. I was not amused.

"Well," I said, "you look Hairy. So I think I'm going to call you Hairy." Everybody laughed. John patted me on the back. "Alright Gus, that's fine. Hey, let me see those G.I. Joes. It looks like Sylvester over there has a machine gun, and Cedric better get behind something."

"You're weird, Hairy." The Muttley laugh started, and it would endure for more than three decades.

• • •

I think my wife drove us to the graveside, but I am not sure. I was embarrassed that I could barely shoulder my share of the burden of carrying the casket. I kept my head down, partially to avoid eye contact, but also so that I would not have to see the unbearable pain of my sister, my nephew and my niece.

When we had placed the casket onto the gurney straps over the grave, the finality of it all hit me once again. We pallbearers had been instructed to remove our boutonnieres and place them on the casket in a final walk by. I was last.

As I set the carnation carefully in its place, I stopped and placed all five fingertips of my right hand on the cold metal. I thought about the things we'd left unsaid and the lack of closeness we'd had in recent years. I felt an emptiness I still have trouble putting into words. I'm sure no one heard me when I leaned down and said, "I love you, Hairy." And then I cried again.

• • •

After that first visit, John became a fixture around our house. He was so different from anyone in my family. In addition to the wild appearance, he drove a bright yellow MG convertible. Even as he advanced professionally, he held onto that car, and years later, when I was old enough to reach the pedals, he'd take me for rides. When we were just far enough down our country road to be out of sight of my parents, he'd pull over, switch seats and let me air out that five speed. It was stupid and dangerous and we could have gotten in so much trouble, but to a 13-year-old, it was an incredible high of freedom and power and getting away with something. He would laugh and shake his head as I'd grind the gears or miss a shift. We never told a soul.

A few months after that first meeting, John and Carol got married. I was the ringbearer, and all the men wore white tuxedos with black trim, and ruffled shirts. My mama still has the photograph of the wedding party on her wall. The flash triggered John's photo-gray lenses, and honestly, we all look like rejects from the wedding scene of *The Godfather*.

• • •

When the graveside service ended, the family went back to my sister's house. It now seemed overly large — all at once, huge and empty and void. I didn't want to talk to anyone, and I headed down the hallway to the bathroom. In a magazine rack, I spotted a Carolina basketball game program.

I didn't have much interest in sports until John came along. One of the first questions he asked me was which college sports team I favored. In the 1970s, in North Carolina, that meant just two choices —the UNC Tar Heels or the NC State Wolfpack. I told him I didn't really know, most of the family didn't care, but they sort of seemed to pull for the Wolfpack.

"C'mon, Gus, you're smarter than they are," he said. "You can do better than that." He was passionate about basketball and was determined to educate me. Over the months and years that followed, he took every opportunity to share the mythology of Carolina basketball — Coach Dean Smith was Zeus, and Phil Ford, Walter Davis and Charlie Scott were Apollo, Ares and Poseidon. I learned that you watch the game on TV, but turn the volume down and listen to Tar Heel Radio play-by-play announcer Woody Durham to get a real feel for the game. Just behind UNC on the sports hierarchy was Boston Celtics basketball. I heard all about John Havlicek, Dave Cowens, Bob Cousy, Bill Russell and and countless others. This was yet another easy connection for us, as Celtic great Larry Bird came along in my generation, and became my favorite athlete

John introduced me to playing sports, insisting that competitiveness could overcome any lack of talent. I eventually figured out that in high school he was a scrawny, nearsighted guard who fought for all of his playing time. Basketball became my love, and he constantly preached the virtues of quick release jumpers, the importance of backspin and the shooters touch, and how to strategically use elbows, aggressive box-outs and whatever other means necessary to combat bigger and stronger adversaries. I collected a lot of bruises before I could ever beat him one-on-one.

• • •

"Don't fade away when you shoot. You'll be short on your shot every time."

"You're a big boy. Use that to your advantage."

"Pump fake, get your man in the air, then shoot when you're on the block. And learn to hit your free throws."

These are the instructions I'd hear, against a backdrop of a ball pounding into the hard packed dirt in my yard, John dribbling, daring me to try to take the ball. If I reached in, I'd get a shoulder in my chest, he'd sidestep, release and then there would be a swish.

Games were always to 11, make-it-take-it, win by two, call your own fouls, but they better be serious. My age — preteen, early teen, then freshman — had no bearing on the games, and I was shown no mercy. I had a losing streak to rival the Washington Generals.

Every Sunday during college basketball season, regardless of how cold it was outside, John would give the word and we'd head out to the barnyard at halftime. I laced up and raced out the door, dribbling, right hand, left hand, just like John showed me.

"Rotate the ball in your hands and follow through."

"Box out."

"Watch my chest, not the ball. I can do anything with the ball, but my chest is going with me."

"Create some space to get your shot off."

Around eighth grade the games started getting really physical, the pushing and handchecking a little tighter, the box outs more enthusiastic. The scores tightened, but I rarely won. The man could not get much elevation, but his position, the fact he was always squared to the basket and ready to shoot, and the way he protected the ball made him tough to defend, and games usually ended on a 20-footer that never seemed to touch the rim.

Then, one year in high school, I grew three inches over the summer and got contact lenses. That, along with his coaching over the years, my growing competitiveness and John's inevitable slowing down, converged and things changed. I started hitting the jumpers, backing him into the lane, blocking shots and winning games. Looking back, he could have gotten angry, but he continued to play hard and even when I wanted to gloat a bit, he would smile and say, "But can you do it again?"

While I know he thoroughly enjoyed beating me over the years, I know too, that like any good coach, he was proud. Not coincidentally, that is when he started treating me like a man, more so than a boy.

• • •

I was with my wife and kids at the fall festival at my church when I first heard about the accident. My niece told me that John had fallen on the steps of a condo in South Carolina, and had been hurt bad enough to go to the hospital. That seemed strange, as John wasn't one for accidents, but I guessed we'd all have something to tease him about when he got home.

He had gone on a yearly golf trip with his core of buddies — all lifelong friends and scratch golfers who spent months picking resorts with the toughest courses for a three day tournament. This was also somewhat of a celebration for him as well. After years of working as VP of manufacturing at Barcalounger Furniture, a company that made the most comfortable recliners and sofas in the world, he was set to become President at the end of the year when his longtime mentor retired. He was stressed, but excited.

The next day, Mama called me early to tell me that John's fall was a lot more serious than anyone had thought. He was in the hospital and he was not conscious. Carol and my niece had driven down, and the outlook was not good. When he had fallen, he hit his head on the concrete landing.

There were a lot of phone calls and prayers made over the next couple of days, each one bringing more grim news. Finally, there was the last call.

"John died."

• • •

At the start of the 1981-82 college basketball season, John called one night. He asked me if I had any interest in going to see Carolina play in old Carmichael Auditorium. It might have been a meaningless game against Citadel, but I was excited to see players I'd only watched on television — James Worthy, Sam Perkins, Matt Doherty and a freshman from Wilmington named Mike Jordan. Carmichael was on its last legs, as the era of big arenas with skyboxes and big money was pushing out the old barns of Tobacco Road. The seats in Carmichael were wood and painted wrought iron, and the crowd was right on top of the players. They still kept a flipchart scoreboard in one of the corners of the court, where a student recorded each basket by hand. Everything metal had seen several coats of blue paint. The hot dogs were good and cheap. The place was hot and smelled like a sweaty high school gymnasium. The fans were loud and intense.

In the decade that followed, we went to many games and never saw the Tar Heels lose. While it wasn't quite the same atmosphere, it was still an event when the team moved into their new domed arena. We even saw the Heels win at Duke's Cameron Indoor Stadium two years in a row, a madhouse where we were bold — or dumb — enough to wear our UNC shirts. The "Crazies" did not enjoy the enemy in their presence, and I distinctly remembered getting hit with pieces of raw carrot and a few plastic cups late in the game that second season. John loved it.

What was more important were the rides to and from Chapel Hill, which was about an hour and a half away. By then, John had upgraded to a long Chrysler LeBaron with huge, plush leather seats. I had dropped "in-law" from my mentions of him — he was my brother. While I hated the soundtrack of his beloved beach music — the Embers, Clarence Carter, Chairmen of the Board — I still remember the smell of that car, the dashboard lights, the old back roads and shortcuts, but mostly the stories. He would talk about the games he played in, Mickey Mantle, Yogi

Berra, sports strategies, hangouts at Atlantic Beach, history and politics and the importance of college.

. . .

I did not see John much at my folks' house on the weekends like I used to. He was busy with work, and my wife and I had three children under 10 as well as a business to run. Circumstances kept John and me apart.

But things were looking up for Carolina basketball. Tyler Hansbrough had established himself as an old school UNC player, and I saw John for just a minute at church one Sunday early in the fall.

"Hey dude, let's go see the Heels play, this might be the year," I told him. "It will be like old times."

John didn't hesitate. "That sounds good, Mike. I'll talk to a guy this week about tickets. Let's do it." Then he did something strange, something he hadn't done since I was a little boy: he patted me on the shoulder. The moment passed quickly, and he was out the door, headed to work. It was the Sunday before he died, and it was the last conversation we had.

. . .

The Tar Heels went on to have a monster season in 2008-09, and capped it by winning the NCAA National Championship. Hansbrough broke just about every ACC scoring record on the books, and none of the tournament games were even close. I watched the championship game on TV and thought about how much John would have savored the win.

That was the last time I watched college basketball with a purpose. It is painful now, because all of my sports interest and background is intertwined with John. I've become almost indifferent to Carolina Basketball, a thought that at one time would have been heretical.

My sons are starting to play basketball and enjoy watching sports on TV. They are about the age I was when John came over that first night to meet the family. I need to make memories with them, take them to some games and let them experience those moments of wide-eyed excitement, and let them see the special things happen in those arenas, on those courts. I need to beat them in one-on-one while I can. I owe my boys that, and I think John would be disappointed in me otherwise. He'd say, "Gus, you're better than that."

• • •

16

Heart of a Wedding

People say things to photographers at weddings that they shouldn't.

It would be impossible to count the number of times that I found myself trapped in rooms with bridesmaids or groomsmen who watched guests come by and remarked about who was sleeping with whom, who had various conditions involving their private parts, and who hooked up at the rehearsal dinner the night before.

"There comes Bobby and his wife and baby," said Bridesmaid 1.

"She's fat," said Bridesmaid 2.

"The baby or the wife?"

Snickers.

"Lord knows that could have been my baby," said the bride. "Mmmmph!" and "Lawd!" echoed across the room.

Mothers of the bride have met me at the door, imploring me to deliver venom-laced diatribes to the mothers of the groom regarding not just photographs, but dresses, flowers and reception arrangements.

I've seen brides and their mothers hissing at each other all day long when no one was watching, while standing arm-in-arm every time a guest or camera was in sight.

Brides have sweated out pregnancy tests in restrooms, hid airplane bottles of liquor in their bodice, told me about their plans (or lack of) for the wedding night, and I learned there *is* such a thing as a maternity wedding dress.

My wife and I eventually got to the point we stopped telling stories; no one believed them. Weddings are the great equalizer in society: money, class, race, culture and location don't categorize a good or bad wedding. We often said we should write a book, take the notes of all the crazy things we saw, and get them published one day. One day long after we decided to retire.

• • •

My sportcoat sleeves were about an inch too short and the collar on my white dress shirt threated to make a deadly projectile out of the button. A poorly knotted necktie and dress shoes that pinched my EEE-wide feet and several pounds of camera equipment completed my burden. I held a Hasselblad camera body, an 80mm lens, a grip, a Vivitar flash with sync cable running to the lens, and a power cable running to a lead-encased battery fastened to my belt — a battery that I was sure was sterilizing me as I stood in the church vestibule.

My jacket pockets were loaded with rolls of 220 Fuji professional film and detachable backs for the cameras. In the pre-digital age of the 90s, rolls the size of shotgun shells fed into a magazine about the size of watch box. My camera could fit 24 2 ¼ x 2 ¼ images onto a roll before the dark slide went in, the roll was wound down, a paper seal licked, and another fed in to replace it. A big affair might require that three of these backs be kept loaded at all times.

The Methodist church organ rumbled to life, the bride and groom came power walking down the aisle, and just before I snapped the photograph, an older couple almost knocked me down as they exited the back row and stood near a door.

The groom extended a hand towards the man, and grabbed the man's shoulder with the other.

"Mom, Dad," said the groom, "I want you to meet my new wife, Deborah."

"Hey, guys," I said, remembering that the groom had told me in the consultation that his parents were 'no longer with us,' "how about we get a nice photograph of the four of you together?"

The older woman turned to me, immediately switching from the look of sweet grandmother to the witch who cast the spell on Snow White. "I don't think so."

I felt myself slowly turning red, from the back of my neck, all the way up to my forehead. Even though we were inside, the June humidity seemed to condensate just above my brow. The pause was awkward. No one spoke. A question flashed in front of me: why am I here? I fought it back. "Alright, then. I'll be over there if you need me."

I was 45 minutes into my first wedding.

• • •

My life as a photographer was not a dream come true. There are not photographs of me as a child with a camera around my neck, and I didn't convert a bathroom in our farmhouse into a darkroom. I enjoyed my first camera, a Kodak Instamatic, but photography was far from an obsession.

Later on in high school when I started working part-time as a sports correspondent, the local sports editor put a Pentax K-1000 in my hands. It was an all-metal, practically indestructible 35mm camera. He told me to shoot a roll of film while I was the game, and I could pick up an extra $15 for each photograph that was published. There was also a caveat: I would get one roll of bulk film, roughly 20 frames, to get a publishable image. Any week I came up empty would be my last week with the camera. I took helmets to the lens from linemen and running backs, holding on to the last minute to get the impact shots when plays spilled over the sidelines, and I could anticipate when a safety was going to move up to crush someone, or when a wide receiver was going to stiff arm or run over a linebacker. Basketball was more dangerous, because you could lose the ball looking through the lens, sitting behind the backboard, and the next thing you know a sweaty but scrappy point guard was in your lap. I learned quickly what settings I needed on high school football field, with a 135mm lens, and what worked well in the darkest of gymnasiums — most are so poorly lit, it was aperture wide open and ISO cranked to 250 to stop the action. Positioning and pre-focusing were essential, as was patience. Every week, the staff photographer or an editor would give me advice on how to fine tune my work. It was fun to illustrate my stories, but for me, the magic was in the writing.

• • •

One Saturday, my wife and I pulled up at the country church for a 3 p.m. wedding. There was a hearse parked out back, under a giant oak tree. As I parked my car in the gravel lot, Kristi checked my cellphone to see if I had missed a message.

Before we could check and see if the wedding had been bumped for an unexpected funeral in the congregation, two large men wearing tuxedos piled out of the front doors of the hearse, as did a Jack Russell terrier puppy. One man swung open the tailgate of the vehicle. Instead of a casket, there were stacks and stacks of multi-colored cardboard boxes containing bourbon, gin, rum and about five different varieties of beer. A cooler was pulled out, filled with ice and stuffed with beers.

"Wow," Kristi said.

It gets better I told her, now worried about a comment the bride had made to me two days before. She was a professional clown, and told me that if the inspiration struck her just right, she would be coming down the aisle in full makeup.

Kristi put her forehead on the back of her hand, leaned on the door and just laughed. She knew I hated clowns.

The clown nose stayed in the makeup bag, but that didn't make things uneventful. As I was lining up the large group at the altar, I heard a commotion and then gasps. The dog was loose in the church. Kristi emphatically whispered to me, "Mike!" I looked out from behind the camera to see what I was missing. The Jack Russell dove onto the bride's train, circled, paused and then squatted. Bridesmaids squawked and then a large black dress shoe whizzed by, just in time.

"Bubba!" someone yelled. "Why in the world did you turn that dog loose in the church?"

"It was too hot for him out in the hearse," Bubba said.

• • •

Despite the low pay and long hours of the newspaper business, I loved it. I took a salary cut to become a "communications specialist" in the public relations department of the local school system, but for the first time in my life I had health insurance, paid vacation, sick days and a retirement plan. The things you supposedly need in place to start a family. Kristi and I had been married for three years, and she had just gotten a promotion at the county department of social services. But we were square pegs in round holes.

After years of pursuing truth in my work, developing a watchdog conscious and the youthful cockiness that comes with self-righteousness, I was now in the business of spinning negative truths, such as making falling SAT scores into a positive thing. Witnessing the wasteful spending turned my stomach. There were countless times that I found myself participating in acts that the newspaperman side of me wanted to slap on the front page, above the fold, as scandal.

Kristi's heart was way too big to be working at social services. She carried each of her client's burdens in a bundle on her back, oftentimes coming home in tears because of situations that broke her heart. It is an unseen culture in America that is served by social services — one that neither conservatives nor liberals have a clue about dealing with. The machinations that run the system grind up workers like sausage.

By a certain standard, we were doing all the right things — working professional jobs with benefits and room for advancement. By sticking it out, in a couple of years we could probably upgrade from our mobile home to a house and start a family, something we were starting to talk about. At 24, though, we were both horrified by the "lifers" we worked with in our respective organizations. Lifers go into jobs not considering how much of their life they will give, putting in time for better days down the road, and then realize after a certain number of years that they are trapped. They've invested too much time, have too much set aside for retirement, and have too few broad skills to go elsewhere. They live for 5 p.m. on Friday, and die every Monday morning.

• • •

There are some weddings that you simply know aren't going to work. The bride and groom hardly speak, or when they do, it is curt. The groom checks out every tight-fitting short skirt that walks by at the reception, or the bride gets trashed and hangs out with her friends all night.

Among the hardest weddings to photograph is a second or third wedding for a groom or bride, when you were at the previous ceremonies in the same capacity. Once, a bride brought in her album from her first wedding.

"This is what I want," she said.

"Okay," I replied. "We can work with those same ideas."

"No, I mean I want it just like this. I love this book. I want the same poses in the same places. If you want to take this to the wedding, you can." The location, outfits and participants — other than the groom — were exactly the same. Literally. The bride wore the same dress, as did her mother, from the previous wedding. She didn't even bother to have a new bridal portrait made, even though years had passed; she instructed me to simply remove the date and replace it with the current year.

One year, we photographed a groom's second wedding and his ex-wife's second wedding. I couldn't tell stories, make jokes, or talk about the past. Kristi spent the day as my handler, and advised me to just for one day, keep my mouth shut and do my job, be professional and go home without an awkward moment.

On Saturdays after weddings, especially before we converted our studio to all digital, it would take hours for me to get to sleep. I stayed up until 2 a.m. or later trying to wind down. I was tired and sore from standing on my feet for eight hours straight, but the mental exercise took a heavier toll. I watched movies, had a glass of wine, and then finally crawled into bed. My mind raced. Did I get all the shots? Did the flash sync correctly every time? Did I have the exposure right? Were everyone's eyes open? Was everything sharply focused? When I finally did go to sleep, all kinds of scenarios played out: the shipper would lose my film, the processor would accidentally expose the rolls, and I'd lose a film back with the roll from the ceremony. Or the cake cutting. Or the parents. It was the same thing after every event.

Things got better with digital. I went home and made backups of all the disks, and knew instantly that the job was in the bag.

However, digital was far from foolproof. One night, I pressed the wrong button on the camera and erased an entire disk of images. It was the disk with all of the family photographs from the church up through the cake cutting — the heart of the wedding. I felt queasy right there on the edge of the dance floor, knowing I had ruined the day, failed at my job and let down one of the most gracious families we had ever worked for. As I turned to go to the door for some air and a prayer, the mother of the bride put her arms around me, squeezed me tightly, kissed my cheek and whispered, "You did so much to make today perfect. Thank you, thank you, for being here. I know the album is going to be beautiful." I left like a cheat and a pretender, fought back the rising nausea and hugged back.

That prayer was answered at 1 a.m. when after an exhaustive Internet search, I found a software program that could recover the images from the disk, one-by-one in a slow, time consuming process. At 4 a.m., I crawled into bed after salvaging 119 out of 121 shots. When I woke up the next morning, I hurried to the computer to make sure it wasn't a dream and found that I had made five backups of the wedding.

. . .

For our publications at the school system, we shot black and white film. Because we needed a quick turnaround, we had our film processed by the owner of a local studio in Nashville. I delivered the film, and then returned a few days later for contact sheets or to select what we needed for prints.

I built a friendship with the photographer, Ben, and over time, shared with him how my job was becoming less writing and photographing and more catering and schmoozing. Sometimes, I arrived early and we'd have to wait for contact sheets or film or prints to dry and I watched him build custom frames, make prints for other clients or talk about making better photographs. He seemed to enjoy his work. Whether he made portraits and photographed weddings, copied old photos or cut mats, he was creating things, real things, true things. His wife's watercolors hung in the front lobby alongside his black and white fine art work, all lit by spotlights, the closest thing the county had to an art gallery. He always seemed to have more work than he could do.

One day, after a particularly long stretch of frustration at work, I knew it was time for some changes.

"Ben," I said, "I'd really like to talk to you about a job after Christmas."

Ben was working on a frame and didn't respond.

"I don't care what it pays, I just have to do something different," I continued.

Finally, he spoke. "How about instead of coming to work for me, you just buy this place?"

"Mainly because I don't have any money. And, I know nothing about studio photography."

"We can work those things out. I'll even stay a couple of months and show you how to do stuff. I've been wanting to move back home for awhile now, and this might be just the thing we both need."

On April Fool's Day, 1996, I closed a deal for my own photography business. Ben was late getting to work that day, so I couldn't do much. I didn't know how to load a medium format camera, make prints or put a frame together.

• • •

A beautiful lady came in for a formal bridal portrait. The session went well, and her, her mother and her sister and I all hit it off well. As they were preparing to leave, there had been no mention of the wedding, and I wondered why she hadn't brought it up. So I asked.

"Oh," she replied, "We would have loved for you to do the wedding. But it's going to be in Mexico. Our family loves Cancun, and we're getting married on the beach."

"We'd go to Mexico for you," I joked.

About three hours later, the bride called the studio. Would you really go to Mexico to photograph our wedding, she asked. Because if you're serious, get us a price. Kristi thought I was full of it, but called AAA. Before the day was over, we had plane tickets and accommodations and I was looking up rules, regulations and tips for traveling safely with film. It was an unbelievable trip, as we made images on the beach for three days, and then enjoyed two days of pools, hot tubs, sightseeing and pampering — essentially the honeymoon we never had.

A year later, we got another job out of the country. This time the destination was the Bahamas. It is hard not to be inspired when your drive to the wedding location was literally the same one James Bond took in *Thunderball*. We were now international pros.

Not all weddings had to be exotic to be rewarding. There was a wedding at a lake two hours away from the studio, where just days before a hurricane had wrecked the place. Telephone lines and power were out, and we drove up to the North Carolina-Virginia line not knowing what to expect. The wedding party and the families had been without power and showers for over 24 hours, but made the best of it, never complaining. It was a hot, late summer wedding, and power was restored just in time for the reception guests to get a late, but very nice dinner. As we prepared to leave that evening, the bride kissed me goodbye and slipped something crumpled up into my hand; I knew it was money. I protested, but she leaned into my ear and explained to me that was the way things worked where she was from, and that my refusal would be insulting to her and her father. Confounded by how to handle a tip from the bride, I finally stuffed the bill into my pocket. An hour down the road, when I stopped to get gas, I remembered and thought I better stick the money in my wallet so I didn't lose it — it was a single bill with Ben Franklin on one side. I'm still embarrassed a decade later when I think about how the bride who had her wedding planned a certain way, saw it turned upside down, but wanted to make sure we were treated properly.

• • •

It is amazing how much better a person can focus when groceries, mortgage payments and car payments are on the line. In 60 days, Ben had me operational in all aspects of the studio. Weddings were just a small part of things, he assured me, but offered a built in generator for the bread-and-butter of a small studio — children's portraits. This made up about 70 percent of our business.

When the employee that came with the business left after 90 days, Kristi quit her job and we became partners. Many remarked over the years that they could never work with a spouse all day. It was the opposite for us. We had a special relationship, particularly then, and we loved being together all the time. I think that clients picked up on that as well. Business improved every month. It was a gift to be able to sit down together for all three meals a day, and to be free to create. For Kristi, the rock filled backpack was thrown off. We thought it would always be like that.

• • •

We designed and built our house at the turn of the century. The business was growing by leaps and bounds, and we found ourselves trying to keep up. We were slightly underpriced among our competitors, trying to catch up from the price list we had inherited. For all his amazing talent, he was giving work away. That is a common malady in the photography business, as in all the arts — the lack of confidence by the artist to ask in fees what he or she is truly worth. We lived modestly, assuming we had to pay our dues.

• • •

While every woman is different, brides do manage to place themselves into distinct categories. Planning a wedding can change someone.

For every 25 wonderful brides, there is one that is "Fatal Attraction" crazy. She can come in many forms: a referral, a cold call, a bait-and-switch sweetheart or one you saw coming, like a freight train that makes you freeze in the tracks before it runs right over you.

She is the bride who gets falling down drunk at the reception, doesn't remember being asked if there anything else she needs before the photographer leaves. She is the bride who refuses to select the plan she needs, instead buys the cheapest plan, thinking she can trick you into giving her a bigger one after the fact. She is the one who, after being unable to trick you, goes on the Internet after she gets her album and trashes you with a Google review. She is the bride who, despite having lived with the groom for three years, slept in his bed the day before, is horrified at the notion that he might see her in her dress before the ceremony.

Sometimes, it is the mother of the bride who takes this role. She picks a fight with the bride, or sometimes the mother of the groom. She sends you a nasty email after the wedding about all the photos you didn't take that she wanted, even though she never showed up for any meetings with the bride. She refuses to move an outside wedding indoors, even after a thunderstorm rips through the proceedings and blows the altar and many of the flowers into the next county, and doesn't understand why you didn't take the usual photographs at the scene of the wedding after it was over. She is the one who roars into the studio to complain about the items she didn't receive from the wedding, while standing in front of you quoting from another photographer's price list.

Despite their rarity, these are the weddings that lodge themselves in memory. They nudge out the women who become lifelong friends and loyal clients. They kill the sweetness and the sanctity, the romance of the wedding day, and they don't appreciate the images or the art you try to create. As our children came along, and we found ourselves leaving them every weekend to go be with other families, Kristi and I found weddings working us over just like our jobs had from the previous decade. And we had no more passion for this work than that.

• • •

About the time our first child was born, Mama was hanging up the apron from her third career, the one that came after mother and tobacco farmer. She ran a bake shop, supplying several retail stores, and restaurants with cakes, pies and breads for almost 30 years. Full of the energy and drive of a woman half her age, Mama was already restless at home — so she came to work with Kristi and me.

As our family grew, Mama and Kristi rotated schedules so they both got time with the kids and time at work. We added another employee at the peak of our business in the late-2000s, not long after our last was born.

Our crazy growth had slowed to a consistent level, but things were happening in the industry that would turn it upside down. As we converted to an all-digital format, with a steep investment, more hobbyists were popping up with websites. We focused on quality of work and profitability, finally getting our prices to a level that should have to led a decent living. We had moved to a larger building to handle extra growth.

And then the march started. Two of the county's largest employers moved operations, companies who paid good salaries to our best customers. Big box frame shops moved in. The recession hit, and the county's unemployment rate soared to just under 10 percent, one of the highest in the state. The clients who still had jobs were worried they might lose them, and held off on such luxuries as custom portraits and frames.

Friends and colleagues across the state were closing their studios. Some filed bankruptcy; some simply saw the handwriting on the wall and found other jobs. While I enjoyed photography, and appreciated the storytelling aspect of it, it was not a passion. I could pose and light and retouch and print, make people look their best and make a living.

Things started getting tight, so we started cutting back little things at first. Mama retired and our friend/employee left to work for her husband. That wasn't enough, and Kristi finally had to leave the studio to take a part time job. We moved out of the big studio into a place a little more than half the size. I found myself suddenly alone all day on most days, answering the phone and dealing with clients.

• • •

There was the day I was photographing a bride in an outdoor session when her mother promptly stepped up and slapped me square in the face. A spider she said, revealing the messy splatter in her palm to her horrified daughter.

There was the bride who misunderstood "Show us the garter" as "Show us what you got." And she did.

There were the rookie food managers I had to break in, the ones who did not realize that a crowd of 20-somethings will not go home until the open bar is closed.

There were way too many macarenas and slides, both Electric and Cha-Cha.

There was birdseed, which begat rose petals, which begat soap bubbles, which begat the awful idea of sparklers. Nothing is scarier than a bunch of intoxicated men trying to light each other's crotches on fire — unless it was the groom getting tossed into a snake infested water hazard on the 18th hole.

But then there were other moments.

There was the Pepsi truck driver who told his wife-to-be he wanted to go from the church to the reception on his route truck. The bride, who looked fresh off a fashion show runway, happily agreed. Halfway to the hall, the groom pulled into the parking lot of a restaurant on his route, where he had hidden away a horse drawn, Cinderella carriage with four white horses, for the rest of the trip over. I'll never forget the look on his face, or the look on hers.

There is something to be said about being happy with what comes your way, enjoying the present, and allowing yourself the chance be surprised, to get something you deserve but don't expect. That is the real heart of a wedding. To linger in the moment.

• • •

17

The Last Wedding

I checked the small gray batteries for my camera bodies that I left charging the night before, to make sure they were topped off. I counted out the silver AA Energizer titanium batteries for my flash and Kristi's. I went through as many as 16 at a wedding, and Kristi might need eight more.

I opened the blister packs and put four batteries each into a small, form fitting plastic case. These went in my jacket pocket for quick changes that might be required during the day, such as altar returns, cake cuttings or twilight shots on the reception grounds.

• • •

It had not been a great week.

One client left a portrait in her car all afternoon on one of those 95-degree days, and the print had crimped, much like hair on a humid day. Her husband came in ranting about how his wife had spent a lot of money and the "picture was messed up." He wanted remedy, at my expense, even though it is obvious that archival materials don't magically curl up for no reason.

Another client brought in a custom frame job on Tuesday, was given a completion time of two weeks, and called after three days to see if her "stuff was ready." She was quite annoyed to find out it wasn't.

The previous week, Progress Energy cut off my power for non-payment. I remembered paying the bill, but the company had applied my payment to the wrong account number. It took an hour on the phone to correct the situation.

Two prospects called to check prices, and complained about how expensive photography was, when all they wanted was a disk they could use to print from an online service.

Like most self-employed people, I had never been great at leaving work at work. My creativity had been subjugated by day-to-day drudgery.

• • •

After packing the batteries, it was time to format the memory cards. Some people delete the images on a card after making a backup, but for longevity and to avoid corruption of files, it is best to reformat each small, black chip, and give it a sort of deep cleaning.

I popped each card in the camera, closed the door and hit the play button, watching the work of the previous week flicker onto the LCD on the back of the camera briefly. With the push of another button, the images would vanish, little girls in all white on wicker furniture, businessmen in dark suits and fashionable ties, high school seniors leaning against their cars — all gone in a instant, the moment erased, room made for someone else's memory to be recorded.

• • •

People call it a midlife crisis. A bump in the road of life can cause not just a flat, but total the whole thing. Looking back, I wasn't having a midlife crisis. I needed to change one path for another. I didn't want a sports car,

I still had a thing for my wife, and a lot of things to do, if I could just figure out what they were.

. . .

Clean lenses are always important, especially with professional glass like Canon or Nikon or Carl Zeiss. The way the optics are designed and sanded and polished and coated produce a clarity and sharpness to the images you can't get in consumer lenses. Since the digital age began, not only do lenses have to be cleaned, but the sensor inside the bottom of the camera body has to remain pristine as well. Something as small as a particle of dust in either place results in a black splotch on every photograph, and lots of touch-up time in Photoshop later. This is a detail to not be overlooked.

I used my best old cleaning cloths on the lenses, careful to gently make sweeping circles on my workhorses, the 24-70mm and the 70-200mm. These pieces have been in my bag for years and served me well, dependable and solid. Caring for them is no chore.

I tucked the telephoto into a sturdy hiking bag, padded on all sides, and neatly divided into compartments, buffered by the flashes, sun shades and accessories. The other lens would go on my favorite camera and into a different bag, later, to be pulled out at one last wedding.

. . .

I asked myself what I would do if I could start over, or if I just locked the door to the studio one day and never came back. I had obligations; it wasn't so simple to land another job after a decade and a half out of the market.

I was still freelancing as a writer, and had steady work, but thought I needed some development. I started looking into English graduate programs. I stumbled across the creative writing program at East Carolina University. When I contacted the school, I discovered that the director of the program was a subject I had written about for a music magazine four years earlier. ECU was 45 minutes down U.S. Highway 264 East, and most of the classes I would need were held at night. A couple of hours after starting my search, I texted Kristi:

"What do you think about me going to graduate school?"

She replied, as she had so many times over the course of our marriage, "I'm for whatever you think you need to do." Then, "What would you do?"

"English. Creative writing."

"Cool."

• • •

I made a checklist of things I would have to do to gain admission to ECU: transcripts, letters of reference, a portfolio, application, and the GRE.

I cringed when I ordered my transcripts from my undergrad time at Barton College. Even though that part of my past was 20 years old, my underachievements were glaring. I felt I had squandered my parents' financial sacrifices when I was an undergrad.

Finding three references was going to prove to be the biggest challenge, as many of my instructors had retired or passed away. One who was still around was my English Composition professor, Dr. Rebecca Godwin. She agreed to meet me and still had my grades from my freshman year. We sat in a crowded Starbucks in Wilson, and I knew she was having a hard time trying to recall my unimpressive performance in her class. Dr. Godwin is the type of professor every parent should wish for his/her child to have; she is tough but fair, a stickler for details, kind, compassionate, and most of all, encouraging. She is the Southern Belle, remade, not with a taste for magnolias, mansions and social calendars, but instead dripping with the sweetness of Faulkner, Lee Smith, Sam Ragan, and Robert Morgan.

"Dr. Godwin, am I too old for this?," I asked. "If I've waited too long, tell me. You'll be doing me a favor."

Without hesitation, she said, "You know what, Mike? In two years, you will be two years older regardless of whether you get a masters or not, so why not? I won't lie and say it will be easy to get a job teaching English, but people have said that for decades."

• • •

My wife and I told no one about the crazy application; it would save a lot of embarrassment if I didn't get in. The studio continued to contract.

The digital revolution had changed many things. The prices of cameras had dropped drastically over seven years, and many amateurs were undercutting prices and "going into business." Hardly any bothered to get permits or remit taxes, most had spouses with jobs to support their families, and most turned out awful work. Professional labs, once the gatekeepers of high standards, started relaxing account requirements. Facebook posts made images that would never print well look wonderful, especially on high-resolution monitors.

I was starting to feel tired. When we first started, Kristi and I would sometimes work 28 out of 30 days in a month to build our business. My philosophy had been build now, enjoy the benefits later. We took jobs and clients that cost far more in money and stress than they were worth. By 2008, I had won awards, earned professional degrees, and been president of the state association. I had paid my dues. The only problem was that the reward that was supposed to be waiting turned out to be a mirage. Our slow delivery was no longer equated with waiting for quality, it was an annoyance to many folks. From age 26 to 41, the prime of my working life, we built the business and in one-eighth of that time, it was all unraveling. We had three small children, and a mortgage. The joy of making portraits, especially of children, became something I dreaded. I had less patience, just as clients were becoming more demanding. I questioned the value of what I was doing, and whether I was willing to try to stick it out and make it work.

Then I got an envelope in the mail, with purple and gold letterhead, that began, "Congratulations and welcome to the graduate program at East Carolina University…"

• • •

The manufacturer of my main camera bag markets it as "The Rolling Strongbox." Tough, weather resistant nylon encases a soft, padded interior that has compartments to keep any metal instruments from banging together. With a set of wheels, and a pop up handle, the case looks just like an ordinary airline walk on piece, and fits in an overhead compartment.

Zipper pouches in the top offer room for memory cards, small tools and change. An outer compartment was perfect for programs, and our notes for the wedding day on all the special or out of the ordinary shots. Some pros think a checklist looks amateurish; we always considered it a thorough way to ensure we left nothing to chance at an event that couldn't be reproduced or re-shot. I packed my camera, the extra batteries, my backup camera, my backup flash, everything I could think of, all the things I'd carried over and over again. We'd carry them one last time, I thought as I ran the zipper around the case, for Corrie and Elic.

• • •

The room was small, with a long table. The professor entered shortly, in a herringbone jacket, patches on the sleeves, shirttail out over blue jeans. He sat down, put on reading glasses and maintained a very serious demeanor. Index cards were passed out for contact information, and syllabi went around the table. He gave a brief overview of the assignments, but still no smile. He collected the cards, we made the standard introductions, and then he looked up and promptly dropped the f-bomb. I'd never heard a professor do this, but I knew times had changed. He then went on to explain the origins of the word, and the usage of language. He went to the whiteboard and started explaining writing and literature on a simple diagram where you could fit everything ever written. I was hypnotized. He must have talked for half an hour, and I don't think I blinked. I scribbled pages of notes. By 7 p.m., my brain felt as though it had been awakened after a long nap.

Across the hall in the ancient, fading building was my thesis advisor. He sported a headful of white hair, an impish sense of humor, and immense knowledge of craft. He could instill confidence while pressing you back in a chair with challenges and questions. He introduced me to creative nonfiction, and laid the foundation for my approach to writing — disjoint time, use the Return key liberally, think like a novelist.

It didn't take long before I was looking into MFA programs. I could already see I wanted and needed more. I hadn't realized there might be a career where you teach new writers and have time to work on your own writing. Again, Alex was to the point: an MFA would get a foot in the door for a fulltime college job, but it would take publications and books to get a seat at the table. And then he offered this, which I thought was about writing, but now I'm not so sure: "All that will come. You're only here for a short while. Enjoy it, and get all you can out of it."

• • •

I moved the studio to a smaller, less expensive space. After spending two years paying off credit cards and putting them away, we had to drag them back out. I logged almost a hundred miles round trip to ECU, four days a week.

For the first time, keeping all of our business and personal bills current was a challenge. I used to have such contempt for people who wouldn't pay their bills or stalled or made partial payments; now I was one of them. Kristi and I sold stocks and retirement investments we had spent years building. Just when I needed them most, the local banks I had spent years doing business with suddenly became less flexible, even on the smallest of lines of credit. Fifteen years of paying on time, every time, counted for nothing.

Days at the studio were spent working for money to turn over in payments, then I'd drive to class at night, or go home and read and write papers until 2 a.m. I saw Kristi and the kids less, and when we did have time together, we were mostly tired or irritable.

• • •

I taught a composition class as a teaching assistant that last semester at ECU. The title is misleading; a TA is a student adjunct. I enjoyed the work. I graduated in May 2012, and by the fall had lined up adjunct work at four local colleges. It was a six-course load, a suicide mission.

By taking on the work, I was forcing myself to make some hard decisions regarding the studio. Something had to give. Kristi and I had talked for years about giving up weddings, easily the most stressful and often, least profitable aspect of the business, cleverly disguised by a big, one-time payment from the bride just before the event. We agreed that we would book none for 2013.

The last wedding was a good one. I had first photographed the bride when she was a pre-teen, and her family had been clients for years. Corrie was beautiful and easy to work with. She and Elic were in love, that was evident, and it would be nice to know the last wedding was one we felt would go the distance.

It was an odd feeling folding up the carbon fiber tripod and dropping it and the camera bags in my trunk. I laid my sport coat across the backseat, and Kristi put a couple of bottles of water in the cup holders. The drive to the church was unlike any before. The anxiety wasn't there, and as we moved through the pre-ceremony photographs, the service and the departure from the church, my camera felt lighter in my hands.

The ceremonial dances were danced, toasts were toasted, and the cake was cut. Soon enough, the guests lined the entrance with sparklers that punctuated the cooling fall air and reminded us that winter wasn't far away. The couple hopped in their car and pulled away. We said our goodbyes.

Unlike the hundreds of times before, I took my time repacking and checking my bag in a side hallway. There would be no more short weekends, no more sleepless Saturday nights replaying the events of the day. I knew I'd never be standing in a ballroom again, watching a room of strangers dance and celebrate with their families while someone else kept watch over my young family. It was hard leaving those sad, eager to play faces every weekend.

Photography, as I imagine any self-employment might be, was hard to let go. Photography is personal, because the photographer *is* the business.

This meant the studio would have to be reduced to assets and then sold off piece-meal. This was where the tears would come, the sense of failure manifested. What the heck was I doing? When I should have toasted the end of a successful life stage, a turning of the page, I was instead tangled like a garden hose left out over the winter: one knot released just exposed another.

We had assets to sell, but no matter how the numbers were crunched, it was obvious that when I walked away on the last day, I'd be carrying some debt with me. I was burned out, not just on weddings, but photography in general. After more than a decade and a half, it was all gone, by me in a flash, and I had missed the moment to linger in.

• • •

18

The Road

I don't know for sure if old Livingston was a bootlegger. But here is what I do know: he spent an awful lot of time on his porch, he had a lot of visitors at his old house at the crossroads, and there was a big engine in that old turquoise and white '50s Ford with the tail fins in his yard.

Early one morning, we rode by his weather-beaten bungalow on the way to school and the door to his outhouse had been ripped off its hinges and leaned against the privy. I could have sworn that I saw an odd shaped hunk of metal, with pipes coming out of it, broken and tipped over. I asked Mama about it.

"It looks like Livingston blew something up last night," she said.

"His bathroom blew up?"

"Something like that."

I spent the rest of the trip to Bailey Elementary in deep thought. I wondered if he had been inside the bathroom when it exploded.

"What a way to go," I told Mama.

• • •

My favorite bluegrass band, Balsam Range, has a song that includes the line "if you don't know where you're going, any old road will take you there." It can also keep you there. I've thought many times that I should take this road in front of my house, somewhere, anywhere, and see where it leads. There is nothing special about Old Spring Hope Road, and it can be depressing to come home from a city and watch the development, the progress, drop off as the ditches grow deeper, and abandoned structures, rundown houses, shady enterprises and remoteness envelope me.

. . .

Most afternoons, when it was warm, Mr. Roy would leave his house in the curve and head towards Spring Hope. I always knew it, because of the clomp-clomp-clomp of his brown-black mule pulling the red buggy down the asphalt. I ran towards the road to stare — Mr. Roy was always dressed in a white shirt, black pants, white socks, and black shoes. I waved, and he raised his black porkpie hat with one hand while clucking his tongue at the mule.

I never knew how long it took him to cross the wooden rail bridge, navigate the hills and curves and make it to town six miles away, but it was just before dark each evening when he returned. Sometimes, if we had errands to run in town, we'd see the cart and mule parked at the pool hall, and sometimes, that mule would find its way home with Mr. Roy laid out in the back of the cart, passed out.

. . .

I thought my first car might take me off Old Spring Hope Road. After getting my license, I plodded along in my parents' brown Dodge Caravan, when I was able to get the keys. I saved from odd jobs, farm work, and my first year as a newspaper reporter to scrape up half of the $4,200 price tag on a used, once-wrecked, marshmallow white, 1984 Chevette 5-speed. Mama and Daddy spotted me the balance, provided I drove safely, kept my grades up and got ready for college. One instruction stood out:

"One speeding ticket, and that thing gets parked under the barn shelter," Daddy said.

It was easy enough to keep the car under the legal limit. Once it got to 60mph, it shook terribly and made so much noise I couldn't hear the radio. I had my first date in that Chevette, and it got me through my freshman year of college. It was the car that I drove to see my future wife many nights at Barton College where I commuted my first years.

Shaky as it was, the Chevette got me back and forth without fail, except for once when the timing belt broke and left me beside the road. Once, I got pulled by a state trooper on a back road, headed to class. I think by the time he got to my window, he felt silly; I got by with a warning ticket. I never did mention it, only prayed they didn't mail any notices to the house.

• • •

Spring Hope is located in Nash County, North Carolina, about 45 minutes directly east of Raleigh. Nash County is shaped sort of like the state of Nevada, flipped sideways.

Spring Hope has a quirky history. A man named Crenshaw helped establish the community in the mid-1800s near a series of springs that legend says the settlers "hoped" would never dry up. A post office and stagecoach inn were established. However, the Wilmington and Weldon Railroad ran a spur line from the northeastern city of Rocky Mount to a place a few miles away in 1886. Within a year, a town sprouted around the depot, which they called Spring Hope. There aren't that many towns that just pack up one day and move four miles down the road. The previous village became Old Spring Hope. A store remained there for at least 90 years, and I remember visiting a time or two as a child, but never bought anything. Older folks recall that the proprietor never recorded a sale because "somebody else might come along and want that."

Old Spring Hope Road runs from the county seat of Nashville almost to Franklin County in the south, but it is still considered a back road.

• • •

A couple of years into my college career, I bought a Chevrolet Camaro, a car that went way too fast for the immature boy I was at the time. It is a testament to the protective hand of God that the speeds achieved in that red, low-slung V8 did not come to a bad end. I was far from Daddy's advice on safety; I was invincible, and I was going places and I was going to get there in a hurry. The manual transmission only seemed to encourage this. Ironically, I never got so much as a warning ticket in that machine. I was sure if that Camaro did not take me somewhere away from Nash County, my bride from the Virginia mountains might.

The economic and educational realities of eastern North Carolina were no more promising 20 years ago than they are now. Other than Greenville, with its university 45 minutes to the east, the other eastern counties stagnated. Tobacco markets changed with the end of the quota system, textile mills and furniture makers closed or downsized, and other major employers were bought out and consolidated. The area between the capital and the coast became a pass-through to the beach for those from more prosperous regions such as Raleigh-Durham, Greensboro, and Charlotte.

Despite the advice of counselors and well-meaning family and friends, I was not cut out for business, banking, accounting, or anything agriculture related. My interests were in the written word and the photographic image. That in itself promised I'd need to follow our road somewhere else.

• • •

There was a warty old white woman named Hortense who shook her fist at anyone who walked, biked or drove by her house. Sometimes the hand

172

gesture was worse. There were three country stores at the crossroads less than a mile away from where I grew up. Next door, a black man named Moses beat someone at his house every night. You could hear the yelling. There was the second-generation Lebanese businessman and his wife, a local, who were my parents' best friends and were like grandparents to me. The narrow, meandering, murky Tar River was nearby with the infamous Indian Hole, a whirlpool that took the lives of three sisters on a hot summer day in the 1930s. Some neighbors did not have indoor plumbing, and used a hand pump in the yard to draw water. And there was plenty of cropland.

• • •

Chances came along to take Old Spring Hope Road and not come back. A newspaper offered an editor's job at a resort area in Virginia and another offer came from a college sports radio network.

But work should not be the sole deciding factor for a move. Those jobs never seemed quite right, and Kristi and I stayed put. Five years after we got married, we had a chance to go into the photography business and we took it. We found our niche in self-employment, and we stopped thinking about moving away. We planted deep roots, building a house we sketched out together, a simple ranch that was built on a corner of the family farm given to us as a wedding present. It replaced the mobile home we lived in for seven years, an aluminum tube that seemed as confining physically as road in front of the house had been emotionally.

• • •

When Spring Hope relocated itself to the railroad spur, it saw its boom. The old downtown still exists, and several streets are lined with beautiful examples of early 20th Century architecture. There was a movie theater, a Western Auto, a few farm stores, a dime store, a couple of upscale ladies clothing stores, restaurants, a butcher shop, banks, a couple of garages and full service gas stations, a park, a school, and an old seed store.

Before I was old enough to see over the glass counters, I remember going into the seed store with my parents. It was run by an old gentleman named Duck Sykes, who dispensed carrot, beet, cabbage, corn, bean, squash and many other varieties of seeds with lead scoops, pouring the contents into metal containers and set onto a scale to be sold by the ounce. Once the proper amount was measured, it was poured into paper bags, which Mr. Sykes folded meticulously and tied with twine so no seed would spill or be lost. The vegetable and the cost were handwritten on each bag. Display cases were filled with suspenders, and straight razors and odd devices I was unsure of. I'd ask Mama about those things.

"I think a lot of Mr. Sykes' things in his case have been there since that store opened," Mama said, "and will probably be there when he's gone." Years later, when Mr. Sykes passed away, the stuff was still there. Collectors came in from out of town and bought it all.

• • •

Our neighbors now are different from those I grew up with. The family farm, once filled with cows or corn or soybeans or tobacco, has been partially subdivided and filled with family homes.

There's Mr. Pulley, just down the road towards town. A black man with kind eyes and a lot to say, Mr. Pulley can still be seen welding in his shop, even though he's well into his eighties, making pig cookers or repairing trailers for friends. Not much older than my parents, he calls them "Daughter" and "Son" when he stops to tell them he's been praying for them. Mama always brags that if more people were like Mr. Pulley, the world would be a fine place. Mr. Davis, with white hair that offers a stark contrast to his skin, is a successful self-made beef rancher, landlord and local philanthropist. Late one night when I had a break in my fence and could not keep my young goats corralled, I found myself out of hay. He had his son drive a tractor to my house, in the dark, with a round bale forked on the front. The ride had to be at least one hour round trip in the cold, and the Davises would take no money. Only after insisting was I able to get the son to take home some fresh eggs from my chickens. I'm still humbled by their kindness and generosity.

Some colorful neighbors stayed a while, then moved back home, such the Retzlaffs from upstate New York. They were the talk of the road when they first came down; after all, why in the world would Yankees want to move here? They dropped their guard long enough to learn southern hospitality, and I learned how to play euchre. The exchanges between Daddy and Mr. R should have been recorded as an exercise in cultural diversity: the fast talking, smart-remarking Northerner versus the laid back, homespun Southerner. It didn't take long for them to build a solid friendship.

We still have our share of characters. On Moses' old property, a new neighbor threatened to sue another over some homing pigeons that ate her attic insulation that didn't exist.

There's the mysterious beekeeper down the road, who looks like one of the guys from the duck call reality show, and who once caused my heart to crowd up in my throat when he snuck up behind me after I'd stopped to ask him about some equipment he was throwing away.

"Whoa, Mr. B!" I said.

"Hmm. Didn't know who you were."

"Well, I thought you'd recognize my car, since I live next door."

"I have to lay low because of our mutual neighbor across the road. You know he's a thief. Don't let him in your yard."

"Yeah," I said. "I was wondering if you minded if I picked up those hive frames you've got in the trash pile by the road, next to your trash can."

"That ain't trash."

"Oh, sorry."

"But you can have 'em anyhow. Ain't gonna use 'em no more."

I thanked him, quickly loaded the frames and then noticed what looked like at least 30 hives in his backyard. "Do you mind if I look at your setup back there?"

"Nobody goes back there. Dog might get you and I can't promise I can get him off." At that point, he disappeared. Maybe into the house, maybe into the high weeds on the edge of his yard.

. . .

Only a business or two from my childhood remains open in Spring Hope, other than the banks. Like many areas of high poverty, drug culture abounds, spreading out from Rocky Mount to smaller towns like veins leading away from a major organ. If ever there was a time to consider taking that road to the end, not looking back, and starting over somewhere that is safer and has more cultural offerings for my family, now would be time. I think sometimes it would be nice not to have to drive a half-hour just to get to civilization. We are the last to get electricity restored during hurricane season, and the last to see snow plows during winter. We can't get much delivered, other than the mail, and even that takes awhile.

But.

There is a lot to be said for living in a remote area. We live close to nothing, but we are really not that far from the several good-sized cities. There is something to be said for being able to keep goats and chickens, and to never get a noise complaint from the neighbors. We can shoot and fish and my kids can raise Cain. When it does snow, we have been known to tie kayaks behind pickup trucks or ATVs and drag friends and relatives on the ride of a lifetime. We can see the stars at night, watch the fireflies in the summer and walk the woods in the winter when the brambles and poison have bedded down for the season.

And perhaps just as importantly, when we leave and go down Old Spring Hope Road, we know it will take us back. It will curve and turn and bring us home, a place that isn't that hard to leave until you try.

. . .

19

Let Me Go Ask My Sales Manager

I brought the old copier paper box into the house and set it down on the floor next to my desk, an old roll top I found on Craigslist over the summer for $30. In the box were the hastily-tossed contents collected from my Honda Element the night before, the vehicle I'd said over the years I'd never get rid of until the day she stopped running.

As it turns out, the Element was more loyal to me than I was to her—like a mistress cast to the side after a newer model comes along. She never once left me on the side of the road, failed to crank, got stuck, slid on the ice, or needed costly repairs. But still, I'd stood right there, alone, in a dimly lit parking lot, on an unseasonably cold late September night, putting years' worth of memories into a box while the dealership's business manager happily prepared my paperwork in his office. I figured I'd just go through the stuff when I got home.

• • •

A tub of Clorox disinfecting wipes. Ten validated bank deposit slips. One very thick Carolina Hurricanes winter glove. One ice scraper.

• • •

Why is it that so many things have changed over my adult lifetime, which legally started in the late 1980s, but for some reason, buying a car has not? I can buy any book ever printed without leaving my computer. I can check prices on any item with a few clicks. The veterinarian will come to my house. The doctor will email my prescription to the drugstore. With a few clicks, the grocery store will make my shopping list based on a card I have scanned every time I visit.

However, just like it was when I bought my first car the summer after I turned sixteen—a previously wrecked Chevrolet Chevette—I still have to go through the same system. Salesman and Sales Manager. And when the process is over, I've been leaned on, pumped up, backslapped, left to wait, winked at, done a favor, given the best deal ever, and feel like I need a long shower. Because the business of buying a car is oh-so-dirty.

• • •

One white, narrow box that used to hold baseball cards, which are now gone. My daughter's white and blue hair brush. One 3x5 notecard, with a child's handwriting, listing potential names for puppies.

• • •

I decided to re-invent myself about 18 months ago. Graduate school had been in the back of my mind for almost 20 years. I almost went to East Carolina University as an undergrad, then almost for a history master's in 1992, going so far as a meeting with the department chair. He said to figure on about seven years to finish, part-time. Too long when you're 23. English came up in the mid-90s, with the same timeline. Babies and a photography career came along, but I never stopped writing. Once again, my path crossed with an ECU professor, this time in creative writing.

Three knocks on the door, it was time to answer. This meant a 45 minute-plus commute to class in Greenville, North Carolina, on a great car, albeit one that managed to get just 19 miles to the gallon. By the end of the semester, I started having heretical thoughts. Something had to be done. School was great; $85 a week on gas, not so much. After a summer of selling off guitars and retirement accounts to keep the bills paid, my schedule on campus would double for the fall, as would my fuel bill.

The red Honda Element, paid for when times were good, would have to go. It would not be easy. Red Elements were "short runs," I'd been told by Honda dealers and seen as evidence; only about 5 percent of production that year. In that car, I had become like Norm from the TV show *Cheers*. Everybody in Nashville, where my studio was located, knew me and the car, and every day was like a parade with me waving at folks who could see me coming. It was comfortable, versatile, and dependable. My kids thought it was cool, and I know how quickly the clock was ticking on that mindset. My wife said it was "so you." Pragmatism would have to supplant ego. I started shopping.

• • •

One rain poncho, new in the pouch. Two bug catchers from an outdoor science kit my boys got for Christmas. One collapsible police baton. One coupon for a discount on tires at a store in Wilson.

• • •

I searched the Internet for a possible replacement. New was out of the question; it was a matter of how old would I have to go. Quickly, that narrowed the search to Honda Civic Hybrids or their Toyota counterpart, the Prius Hybrid. I tried to keep this search under wraps, but some of my friends found out and questioned my manhood. Secretly, I became infatuated with these two cars. They could save me money, and confound people who wanted to stereotype me a certain way because how could a conservative love the environment, buy a green car, be for getting our troops home, hate government overspending and waste, be against stimulus spending, be pro-life, anti-death penalty, pro-Social Security and pro-Medicare? It would be so much harder for my liberal friends to go after me and my conservative friends would now have to keep a wary eye on me. Nirvana.

I first spotted a great deal from a dealership in Raleigh, and emailed them for a test drive. Come on down, they said, check us out. We have the best deals around and we treat people right. I took my four-year-old as insurance. Not only is he cute, but far more observant than I; plus, he has no qualms about passing gas, having bathroom emergencies, or threatening a good ol' tantrum with a signal from Dad that *We need out, son.*

We arrived at the nice, modern dealership with a cavernous showroom to drive the Prius with less than 20,000 miles on it and a price tag of $15,000. A salesman glad-handed us at the door and disappeared to get the key. He came back shortly.

"Good news and bad news, Mr. Bradley," he said. "The bad news is we sold the car over the weekend. They just haven't gotten if off the Internet yet. You know, we're so busy and all." There was one other customer in the building. "But the good news is, we have a 2010 model still here that is just $7,000 more."

He actually said that. It takes confidence to reach for a 40 percent increase in a sale in the first 15 minutes you meet someone. He became less cheerful when I asked for clarification: was he going to offer me the 2010 for the price of the 2005?

My son and I sat in the car, and I used my iPhone to pull up another dealership in the city, one that had lots of used Prius models on their website. They advertise constantly on a Raleigh TV station, touting honesty, the best deals in town and not being like the other dealers.

We pulled up in the lot and instantly, out of nowhere, not one but two salespeople descended on us. I asked about the used Prii (this is the plural of Prius, according to Toyota) since they were nowhere to be seen.

The two salespeople split up; one to an office, another back to his desk. He never came back. The first salesman returned and invited us into a high-tech, spotless "branch office" on the sprawling dealership campus.

"Well, we sold those you saw on the Internet over the weekend," he said. "But we have some great 2011 ones out there. We're so busy, we can't keep up with that Internet stuff." I was the only customer in the building. It was 11 a.m. There were eight employees sitting at a table discussing the previous weekend's football games.

I took his business card, the one he forced on me, and didn't look to see if he was still watching when I tossed it in the trashcan on the way out. We left.

"Why are we leaving, Daddy?" Lowell asked.

"Well, buddy, let me tell you about something they call Bait-and-Switch…"

· · ·

One children's book shaped like a John Deere tractor. Six ballpoint pens. One pair of drugstore sunglasses, with the left lens missing.

· · ·

Things weren't much better in the small, scrappier towns of eastern North Carolina either. As we left Raleigh, you could track income levels dropping all the way out to Tarboro. Housing developments were traded for trailer parks, gas and food at exits every few miles swapped out for the endless pines in the median and lining the edges of Highway 64. Even the condition of the roads change as you edge progressively eastward—smooth blacktop dropping off to old rumbly gray dropping off to patched up, cracking asphalt, as if those in the more moneyed parts of the state need reminders to stay away from here unless they're headed to the beach.

In Tarboro, we stepped inside and back in time. Faux wood paneling, popular about 45 years ago, covered the walls of the showroom, which was cramped, messy, and dreary. This dealership bragged about "no-haggle" pricing, which is just a nice way of saying "we don't negotiate." We drove a six-year-old Pries, one that made me wonder if it had been state's evidence once. It wasn't clean, there were mysterious stains and the engine light would not go off. While we were assured it was simply a "sensor" that needed replacing, we weren't buying that story or the car. The offer for my Element was about $2,600 less than the Blue Book value for "barely running." I asked about a reduction in the price of the car. We were assured by a paper "run from the Internets," the saleswoman said—that this car was the best deal for 150 miles. I laughed, shook my head and walked out. Before I got home, there was an email from the sales lady urging me to come back; she had convinced the sales manager to raise his trade-in price $2,000, "just for you, Mr. Brinkley. And, you saw that Internets paper—the Pries is a rock bottom price."

Which brings up another point: does anyone really believe that it is you and the salesperson fighting the evil, office-ensconced sales manager? That you, a total stranger off the street, or the "Internets," has bonded so tightly and quickly that the salesperson feels a need to rebel against the boss—the person who signs his or her check every week—and side with you for The Best Deal Ever?

• • •

A rewards card from an auto parts store. A notepad. A small pouch of tissues. Business cards I never gave out.

• • •

I guess I've never had much patience at car dealerships. The last time I car shopped, I was asked to leave after waiting for an hour for the salesperson to go battle the sales manager. When I walked in their office, they were talking about their favorite TV shows.

"Hey, I hate to interrupt you guys," I said, "but I have things to do. You got a price on my trade?"

The sales manager took his feet off his desk, his hands out from behind his head, and sat forward in his chair. "Well, you've got a V8 and nobody wants those things with $2 gas. You'd have to be crazy to buy one. We can't pay people to take them."

• • •

Having listened to a salesman hammer down the guy in the next cubicle over, pushing a Highlander V8, that by pre-2008 standards got about 12 miles per gallon, I pointed to the other customer. "Have you told that guy?"

"Hey, why is that man pointing at me?" I heard the guy ask.

I stuck my head out of the sales manager's office. "They just told me you'd have to be crazy to buy a V8. They can't give them away."

The sales manager told me I probably needed to leave. On the way out, I saw the Highlander guy get up and follow. It shouldn't have, but it felt good.

• • •

A pack of electric fence clamps. About $8 in change. An empty box for a phone charger.

• • •

I would have bought a Prius in Kinston. Growing weary of the whole process, I lucked out and got a part-time preacher as my salesman, and I laid all my cards on the table upfront.

"You've got what I want. It is the nicest car I've driven since I've been looking. Your price is fair. Give me $9,600 for my Element and I'll drive it home. Trade-in value is $11,000, worst case. Full retail is $12,800."

183

Off to the sales manager.

Surprisingly, back with the sales manager, a man who defied the stereotypes I'd been experiencing. I wanted to like him. I really did.

"Hey, Mr. Bradley. Nobody will buy anything with that kind of mileage, so we're doing you a favor at $8,500. And the deal on this Prius is unreal. Unreal. I can't believe it has been here so long. So can we do business?"

"Gentlemen, I appreciate you being straight," I said, trying to remain, well, straight. "There's no hard feelings on my part, and I'm not trying to be a jerk, but $9,600 is my only offer. It's getting late and we all need to go home. I can drive either car home. You pick."

I drove home in my Element.

The next day, the preacher/salesman urged me to come on back and grab that car before someone else did because there was no way it could be there much longer. I asked did that mean they had met my terms. No.

After I bought somewhere else, the preacher/salesman emailed me and told me he'd gone to bat and got me the deal I wanted. I was in class and couldn't respond immediately. So he left me nine phone messages on my cell, at home, and at work, within a 15-minute span. It was, after all, the end of the month.

In the end, I called an old friend who had a Civic Hybrid on his lot. The same guy I always end up buying from, a friend who did business with me and whose family I know both socially and professionally. I gave him the same offer. He said he couldn't do it. I said okay, maybe next time, and was getting ready to hang up.

"Well, hell, Mike, okay."

So I drove to the biggest dealership in Wilson, and spent a total of about an hour there, including the time it took to clean out my car. Two employees had to spend about 20 minutes apiece with me. And the company made money on both ends of the deal. It really isn't much trouble to buy a car.

• • •

Before I went in to sign the papers, I flipped the tailgate down on my Element. I sat for just a second in the cool air, and the weird, greenish glow of the car lot lights. It was almost eerie with no one else around. I'd had my car longer than I've had two of my kids. She'd been driven to scores of farms, the Stanley Cup finals, to funerals, to bluegrass shows. I'd hauled hay, dogs, and goats in the back, and even briefly considered transporting a newborn calf (she wouldn't fit in the dog carrier; almost, but not quite).

All my stuff, the things I'd carried and those my wife and kids had carried over almost a decade, fit in a small box that sat next to me. We had some good times in that car, and it was always the "date night" choice when my wife and I could get a babysitter. I looked over my shoulder and the black rubber interior seemed clean, empty for the first time since I drove her off the same lot years ago. Was I really feeling sad about a couple of tons of inanimate steel? Was I about to have a weak moment?

"Hey, let's see if we can get that parking permit off the windshield," the salesman said. "Didn't you say that thing was expensive?"

• • •

I drove the Civic home. According to the instrument panel, I managed 42.9 miles per gallon. The salesman said I'd have to learn that driving a hybrid is a little different, and once you learn the tricks, the numbers would just keep going up. I pulled into my yard, drove up the hill, gathered my book bag, and the box of things from the Element. Just as I was about to walk across the yard to the front door, I stopped, balanced the box on my knee and ran my hand through the items. Satisfied, I opened the Civic's left side back door and tossed the ice scraper on the floor. It was chilly out, and I'd need it soon enough.

• • •

20

Arrowheads

I was in the fifth grade before I managed to convince my parents to let me play Little League baseball. All of my friends had uniforms with numbers on the back, and one day a week they all wore them to school. I did not have one.

Coach Aycock did not seem happy to be stuck with a kid two years behind everyone else, so he sent me to right field, the desert wasteland of youth hardball. I spent the obligatory three innings in the loneliest corner of the park, where the chain link fence with the car dealership ad disappeared into the woods, and the foul line wobbled like June Bug, the town drunk.

I was not a good outfielder (all arm, no catch) and I was thankful that during my tenure with Hagwood's Red & White we rarely played anyone who batted left-handed. My best friend Kelly pitched every game, the only 10-year-old who threw a nasty curveball about half the time, alternated with a sneaky fastball. He was unhittable, at least until high school, when his velocity disappeared.

• • •

For their birthdays this year, my two young sons wanted me to take them somewhere they might be able to find some arrowheads. We spent a Sunday afternoon marching across a just-tilled hayfield, on the banks of the Tar River, heads down, and kicked over every pointy piece of flint or quartz with high hopes. It seems fitting that arrowheads are the Native American symbol for alertness. I remember searching the fields of our farm after every plowing when I was their ages, hoping just once to find evidence that Indians had roamed our land. I told the boys it took a lot of searching, a little patience, and a lot of luck to find just one or two of these treasures in a lifetime. We ran out of all three and never did find a point, vowing to return and look again after the first gulley washer of the summer.

• • •

I took a lot of sports photographs, especially baseball, when I worked as a studio photographer. Hey buddy, put your glove on, hold the bat, hop down on one-knee and smile so your mama will be happy. Okay, team photo time. You six in back, you five down Indian-style in front, coaches on the ends. No rabbit ears. Look this way. Three clicks and we're done.

I always knew which ones were right fielders. No swagger. Shy.

• • •

When I was a few years past Little League, I convinced Daddy to let me go plink some targets with his old .22 caliber rifle. I longed to be considered an "expert marksman," which is what one of his medals from Korea had imprinted on it. When I was younger, I used to see the worn, marred wood stock, the blued but pristine barrel, sitting in the gun cabinet and assumed it was the rifle he had used in his war. The first time he let me hold it, I couldn't believe how heavy it was, and to this day, it still feels heavy, heavy like an M-1, a rifle Daddy did carry.

Daddy took dried, hollowed out gourds and strung them on a series of metal bars that were attached to a tall metal tube. This tower resembled a utility pole, but was basically an apartment complex for Martins in the barnyard. Martins are small, beautiful, purple-black birds, which, according to old-timers, eat more than their body weight each day in mosquitoes and other flying insects. Reference manuals dispute this, but I know we had fewer stings and bites after the Martins moved in. The quick, constantly swooping birds seemed to have little patience for sparrows, who became squatters in the gourds. One day, as I headed down the path, I glanced up at the structure and saw a sparrow. I drew a bead. Was it a Martin or a sparrow? I pulled the trigger, knowing I'd miss. Minutes later, as I stood over the beautiful, shiny purple feathers in a pile at my feet, I knew I'd made a mistake I couldn't undo.

• • •

The only way to learn to hit is to get chances. I got just one at bat per game for Hagwood's Red and White, and I usually struck out. But one night, late in the season, my friend Corey was pitching for the other team. He was left-handed, with arms so long they seemed to stop just short of the plate and then the ball was in the catcher's mitt, almost as if he handed the ball to the guy. I never even saw the first pitch. As he came out of his lanky windup for the second one I started my swing, closed my eyes and felt lightning strike the bat. A tingle ran all the way up my arm, the aluminum bat a conduit to my collarbone. I started running, and I ran and ran, standing up as I rolled into third base, by that point hearing the coaches and the parents in the bleachers yell. I scored on a long fly ball.

Coach Aycock walked over and slapped me on the back. "Where's that been all year," he asked.

I looked at him, happy, but hurt at his backhanded praise. I mumbled under my breath, "Sitting on the bench."

• • •

I still have the two trophies I won that year for Hagwood's Grocery. They've outlasted the sponsor, which closed and reopened as a Piggly Wiggly. The next year, we had a new coach, who showed up for practice on a motorcycle with a pack of cigarettes rolled up in his sleeves. He had tattoos and told us he'd been a Marine. He asked us where we wanted to play. I told him second base, a position I'd never played, and he said okay. To this day, I regret not asking to be a relief pitcher. All those lonely afternoons throwing fastballs, moving changeups, knuckleballs at a tiny strike zone marked in tape on the barn door, and I never grabbed that chance to take a fantasy to reality.

We only won two games that year, but I had a great time. I was playing instead of sitting, hitting instead of striking out, in the infield instead of exile. About halfway through the season, league officials found out the coach's son was 14, two years over the limit, which surprised none of the rest of us because Joe smoked, too. The coach quit, no one volunteered to take his place, and they disbanded our team.

• • •

My favorite tree on our farm was the Catawba. The name comes from the Catawba Native American name for totem. In summer, the tree hung full with green leaves the size of large man's outstretched hands, providing plenty of shade. We had a whole stand, three or four deep in some places, across the road from our house, back behind the old chicken coop, bordering the pond.

Sometimes, on a good Sunday afternoon, Mama and Daddy or a brother or sister would tell me to grab my rod and reel and we'd head to the pond. We'd cross the dam that kept a section of backwoods dry, and set up under those Catawba trees. My brothers or sisters would have spouses (or spouses-to-be) or buddies in tow. The cool area under the trees barely filtered the breeze and was just right: too far from the bank to do serious fishing, but just the right distance to keep an eight-year-old from falling in, or getting red clay all over his shoes.

I was most fascinated by the yellow and black caterpillars that populated the Catawbas. About two inches long, slightly fuzzy, with a horn at the end to offer just a bit of menace, these caterpillars were everywhere, usually two per leaf. They made convenient bait, but I rarely caught any fish. This could have been attributed to the bait, or my inability to sit still for more than ten clicks on my brother's Timex. There wasn't enough action in casting and wetting a line with the red and white bobber on the end, waiting for a bream or crappie, or maybe even a catfish, to strike. Inevitably, I would slowly wiggle and fidget and work my way over to the dam to look down the steep grade and wonder what treasures might lay on the forest floor.

• • •

By the time of prep league tryouts, I was all bat, no glove. I watched baseball every Saturday and every Monday night, checked the box scores everyday in the paper and my parents gave me a subscription to *The Sporting News*. Lacking natural athleticism, I used my love of reading to find out what the heroes on my baseball cards did to be great players. I did have power, so I felt safe with the bat, but I flinched on grounders, turning my head to the side, unable to stay down on the ball like Mike Schmidt or George Brett.

At the one-night try-outs, when I got my turn at the plate, the first three pitches came high and hard inside, two of which I managed to dodge and the third drilled me in the left bicep, the red seams biting through my thin t-shirt. Two more came in the dirt.

"You got to swing at something," the batting practice coach taunted. That's when I remembered second baseman Joe Morgan saying one Saturday morning on "The Baseball Bunch" that he hesitated just for one breath to hit the ball up the middle. The next three pitches I hit as hard as I could right back at the pitcher, one over his head, one he caught, and one popped him solid in the right shin, which brought a string of profanities. Someone told me later he was the Methodist minister.

I spent most of the season on the bench. The other two guys who sat on the bench ran onto the field and slid into second base and home plate after every game. I asked them once why they did that. They told me that if they went home with clean uniforms, their dads would know they hadn't played and would beat them. I had seen their dads, and I believed them.

• • •

One Sunday when I was about 12, I convinced my brother-in-law Eddie to walk the farm with me. Under the guise of a nature walk, I lured him to the dam and stood at the rim. I was sure I'd have to trick him to get him to take me down in the bottom.

"Hey, you ever wonder what's down there?"

Eddie walked up beside me and put his hand on his hips. "Why don't we find out?"

We ducked low hanging branches and got nicked by briars. I kept an eye out for my life's desire, arrowheads. We didn't go far that first day, but we found a natural spring bubbling out of the ground, with plenty of animal tracks and scat nearby. Subsequent trips yielded a partially buried wooden spoked wagon wheel, a stash of liquor bottles that must have been fifty years old, and an old crosscut saw, but no arrowheads.

• • •

After years of looking for arrowheads in every field on the farm, I never had any luck. Then, one day, an uncle said he found a boxful after plowing one afternoon. I asked if I could have one. He said he'd given them all to a friend of his.

• • •

In the middle of the summer, my siblings and I walked across the road to the pond, not to fish, but to pick wild blackberries. An old barbed wire fence at the end of the property had attracted several canes of the prickly fruit bushes. I could only pick a short while before getting gashes all over my arms and legs. The berries always seemed sour to me, full of seeds, which my brothers attributed to what they said was crow pee.

Poison ivy eventually covered the bushes, and finally one winter Daddy hooked a chain to the fence and pulled the whole thing out of the ground. I didn't eat another blackberry for thirty years.

• • •

In a plot at the corner of our micro-farm, my boys and I grow three rows of the sweetest blackberries I've ever tasted. In the middle of the summer, when the three of us try to outrun the fading light, we can quickly pick a bucketful, red-purple runny juice the evidence of how many more we could have had smeared across cheeks, ears, necks, legs, arms and clothes.

• • •

Once, after a hard rain, when I was about 14, I went outside to play basketball. Lying next to one of the tobacco barns was a perfectly formed, solid white arrowhead. It rests in an antique cigar box I found at a flea market, where I keep my other irreplaceable artifacts of my youth, such as a 1922 silver dollar and some $2 bills I'm saving for the kids. There is plenty of room to add more arrowheads.

• • •

21

Education Mercenary

The varicose veins in the asphalt of southbound I-95 marked the miles as I fought to stay awake, lulled by the pines and pastures blurring by at 75 miles per hour. Big rigs rattling by and sports cars zipping past close enough for me to see what the driver was having for breakfast jarred my attention back to the road every few miles. Sometimes, I'd exit for a cheap cup of coffee or a splash of water from a clean restroom to restore me.

I made that hour-plus trip on Mondays, Wednesdays and Fridays to join 20 other weary part-timers teaching ENG 100 or ENG 101 or ENG 102 at Campbell University. Thankfully, the considerate department chair spared me from an early morning commute in her scheduling.

On Tuesdays and Thursdays, I headed 30 minutes north of my home for two classes at N.C. Wesleyan, then 30 minutes southeast to my alma mater, Barton College, for one class, and finally to the local community college for a night class.

Six classes at four campuses required more education and paid about 40 percent less than my peak salary when I was self-employed. With fuel at $4 a gallon, I had to work a full day just to pay for gas money. But I was thankful to have the work. I was higher education's mercenary — an adjunct.

. . .

Colleges and universities use a lot of adjunct professors. Budget cuts and the demands of administration to stay in the black have made it so. There are more people who want to be college professors than there are jobs, so many schools are in a great position to get qualified instructors on the cheap. Most college students don't know or care whether they have part time or full time instructors, and parents don't know unless they visit the college's website.

Adjuncts get no health insurance, no retirement, no pay for preparation or grading, and no guarantee of work beyond their contracts — which are usually one semester at the time. This makes it easy for colleges to fill slots, handle enrollment overflow (and shortages) without much of a commitment.

On the other hand, adjuncts typically don't have to attend faculty meetings, serve as advisors or on committees and can move at will to greener pastures. Since most schools keep adjunct loads to three classes or less, a part timer often needs to work at more than one school per semester.

I went to grad school to improve my writing. Teaching was not really on my radar until I registered for classes my second semester and saw that I could fulfill a requirement, and get paid as a Teaching Assistant after completion of ENG 6625: Teaching Composition.

. . .

"Brandy," a dark-haired, baby-faced freshman, was in the first class I ever taught. After she took off the entire month of February, I felt we should talk when she made an appearance just after Spring Break.

"Brandy, don't take this personally, but you should drop my class," I said. "You can't pass."

"Mr. Brantley, I'm no quitter."

"I appreciate that, I really do. Here's the thing: you can't pass. I'm not good at math, which would explain a lot of things about my life. But you've missed two papers. We're only writing three, and then we have a final project. If you make a 100 on both, that leaves you with a 50, which is an F."

"Well, I'm going to stick it out. I know I can do it."

"Think on it. There are worse things than a 'W' on a transcript."

"I'm going to prove you wrong, Mr. Brantley."

Oddly enough, 18 months later, I ran into Brandy on registration day at another college. She recognized me and came over to talk. She showed me her schedule, which of course had my name on it for English. It was awkward, if not a statistical wonder. I suspect she left me and went immediately to the registrar's office to get a Drop/Add form, since she was not on my roster the next day.

I soon learned that a university was rich ground for a writer who also happened to teach writing. At one school, a student who never made a grade above a 'B' sent me an angry email because she could not understand how she did not make an 'A' in the class. A tall, dark, self-described "party girl" who read the campus newspaper in the back row every class for 15 weeks, insisted that if I was truly "fair" I would give her the points she needed to move up to a 'B' because she had "family issues." A strapping lefthander with a 90-plus mph fastball accused me of jeopardizing his major league baseball career for not passing him, even though he failed to turn in his last three papers; and another student who seemed a victim to sleep apnea must have had six grandparents die or go to the hospital, each on a day a paper was due. I had to advise one former prison guard to stop writing about her desire to be naked all the time; tell another student that going to jail for 30 days was not an excused absence; and received at least two papers written partly in text message lingo. In a developmental English class at one college, I lectured for two weeks about the Illustrative pattern of essay. We studied the textbook, we looked at sample essays, I provided handouts and I gave lectures that included a step-by-step guide to completing a two-page paper. "Andre" turned in a stack of photographs with captions.

"Hey, these are great shots, but I'm not sure why you're giving them to me," I said.

"That's my illustrations, Mr. B."

The student next to him, after handing in two assignments with just one or two complete sentences per page, handed in a perfect third paper. I Googled it. He had cut and pasted the first result from Google. The chairman at that school lamented that today's students were too lazy to even steal properly.

• • •

Community college was unlike any other experience. To say classes are diverse is an understatement. Ages may range from 18 to 65. Night classes are filled with mostly older students who work during the day and need a degree for advancement. They've had enough taste of the real world to motivate them in class. There are some slackers, bored housewives, men caught in middle age who never got a degree and are running in place at their jobs, veterans, single parents, parolees and those down to their last chance. The community college system is the Ellis Island of the education world.

About six weeks in, community colleges are credited for enrollment, and more importantly, state funding. Financial aid refund checks go out. This check is made directly to the student, and the amount reflects the difference in the cost of tuition and how much aid the student was eligible to receive.

I started calling this day Magic Money Day. Suddenly flush with cash, many students stop attending class. It seems like a no-lose situation on the surface. The school gets money, the student gets money, the class size shrinks and the real students get more attention. But really, those who take the money only dig a financial hole that becomes extremely deep after just one or two semesters, and they are no closer to a degree than they were before they registered for class.

I enjoyed teaching at my alma mater. I wanted to model those professors who had challenged me, pushed me when I didn't want to be pushed. Every corner of the place returned a memory; I taught in classrooms where I had worked my way through history, English, religion, psychology and other courses. My freshman composition professor became my great friend, cheerleader and mentor, giving guidance on grading, paper topics, methods and expectations. Times had changed, but not her standard.

I never would have driven nearly 500 miles a week to Campbell just for the money. I enjoyed the atmosphere and the students so much there, that it was actually tough to take a fulltime job when I got an offer elsewhere.

Students in one class stayed after to talk about the stories, and assignments and their writing. The jokingly called it "The After Class" as they bounced ideas off me and more importantly, off each other. I enjoyed student writing much more than I thought I could. There was an interesting intersection: I had students who were much more mature than I had been at 18. Here I was a 40-something, and I still had daily doubts about whether I was on the right course. I was not even sure if there *was* something I could do for the rest of my life.

All the time in the car allowed for plenty of thought and introspection with ESPN, contemporary Christian, bluegrass music, Fox News and NPR filtering the thump-thump of the highway as it funneled me home. As I barreled towards the final year of my MFA work, there were days when I had to ask myself tough questions. What made me so sure I could leave one game where I knew the rules, and trade it for another where I knew none of them?

Those questions made for restless nights. But, like Brandy, I was no quitter, even if the math seemed stacked against me.

• • •

"I'm dyslexic, I just thought I should tell you that," said the nervous freshman who had surveyed the on-duty tutors in the room before choosing to sit with me. I had seen her in the Writing Center the day before, and she appeared frustrated.

"Fair enough," I said, not really sure what to say. "I'm Baptist. What now?"

Some of the tension seemed to drop out of her shoulders. She told me she needed help with a paper, one that had been graded a low 'B,' but did not have any corrective marks on it. I immediately understood her frustration and wondered how she was supposed to know what to do, when obviously her instructor had passed the buck to those whose time she considered less valuable. I suggested she read her paper aloud and listen for errors.

"Are you sure you want me to do that?" she asked. "It will take a while."

"Good," I said. "They're paying me by the hour."

It did take a while and I interrupted her often to ask her what she heard. She may have had a learning disability, but she was very bright. We worked for an hour, and then she spent another hour alone, going through notes and revisions.

Most freshman comp classes are too large for students to get much one-on-one help from instructors. Writing Centers carry a stigma among students, just as any type of tutoring might, as a place for the slow, or as a punishment for poor marks. However, most clients were solid students.

I got to see firsthand what frustrated students. I saw carefully worded assignment sheets with clear instructions, and I saw assignments from other professors that I couldn't figure out.

When the student with dyslexia returned weeks later to tell me she had been making A's on her papers, I smiled and congratulated her. It was nice to do for her what my seventh grade grammar tutor had done for me, and what my youngest son, who has dyslexia, is having done for him by his lower school teachers.

• • •

Wherever I adjuncted, students always assumed I had been around forever. Certainly the gray hair around my temples and ears hinted at this. My bluntness and sarcasm, a hereditary trait, can sometimes be mistaken as confidence, which apparently implies tenure as well.

I always tell students on the first day of class to call me Mr. Brantley, word the syllabi to that effect, and write sample headers with that information. Still, most students call me Dr. Brantley or Professor Brantley.

I don't think most of my colleagues care. I've only known one person who was openly aggravated about this, a high-strung, profane, young grad student. Her desk in the shared office was closer to the door than mine, so my students would often come in and ask her if Dr. Brantley was available. Finally, one day, she couldn't take it any longer.

"You let your students call you Doctor Brantley?" she asked, with lots of colorful adjectives. "And, by the way, I'm not your secretary."

"I don't let them do anything. They just do it. I used to correct them, but I finally just gave up. And you should know better than sit near the door."

"Well, you need to correct them. It is unprofessional of you to let them call you that."

"I don't think they know the difference. Some of them don't know a subject from a verb, so I really don't think they care either way."

"Well, I'm going to say something."

One day, one of my good students confronted me after class.

"Dr. Brantley, I came looking you in your office yesterday," he said. "I think I upset another professor. I asked her if she had seen Dr. Brantley. She went a little crazy. She told me you weren't a doctor, you were just a student like her."

"I told y'all that, you know."

"Yes sir, I know. But it made me want to call you Dr. Brantley. I told some other people in class about it."

"Hmm."

"Anyway, Dr. Brantley, you should be careful in your office. I don't think she likes you."

"I think we probably shouldn't talk about this anymore," I said.

"She has a potty mouth, too. Did you do something to make her mad?"

"Yes. I went to graduate school."

. . .

Adjuncts stick together for the most part, but are wary of each other — after all, fighting for that next tenure-track opening is bloodsport.

. . .

The problem with adjunct teaching is that you never know what is around the corner. Some schools hire from their adjunct pools when a full time position comes open, but there are so many educators looking for work, that can't be counted on.

The semesters that I worked as an adjunct were hectic. There was never enough time to do much, and my diet, exercise, and bluegrass music endeavors fell by the wayside. Sometimes, when I left the house, I had to stop and think what day of the week it was: if it was Tuesday or Thursday, it was three variations of Composition I and two variations of Argument Based Research. Mondays, Wednesdays and Fridays meant Composition and American Literature.

But the variety of the different campuses, the different students and the different atmospheres were an education. I had to convince myself that God had put me in certain places for a reason, and some days, that was my only comfort. I realized that the more miles I put on my car, the more distance I put between my new life and the career I was leaving behind in photography. However naïve I might have been when I started the journey, I never believed I was leaving an imperfect world for a perfect one. Many of my clients and fellow photographers could not understand how I could leave a business, and the independence of my own place, a place of creativity, to be "institutionalized." They had it wrong. At the studio, creativity had long ago taken a backseat to survival, with each year yielding little more than the promise of more hard work, more 70 hour weeks, my fate in the hands of fickle consumers. I had the chance to make life more than a grind, I could make it something substantial.

22

Homecoming

I must have been about four or five years old that simmering Sunday afternoon. Mama pulled and tugged to clothe me in the standard issue 1970s boy's dress, all items one hundred percent polyester: wide-lapel sport coat, white shirt, yellow clip on bowtie, brown pants, black socks, and the most narrow Buster Brown shoes made. They pinched my toes and my heels, leaving blisters on both.

We were not going to our regular church, the one Mama grew up in. We were going to Homecoming at the church Daddy's parents attended, Sandy Grove Primitive Baptist Church. Primitive, or Foot Washing Baptists, were a unique splinter in the Baptist pew. They worshipped without music, sung a cappella and didn't believe in the formal training of pastors. Today, the group's numbers have dwindled drastically, with congregations found mostly in the mountains of the southeast.

The one-room church was just a few miles down the road, and Homecoming was the day that mostly ancient members and their descendants attended service and then had dinner on the grounds. The dirt parking lot featured primarily cars from the '40s and '50s. Our Volkswagen van stood out like a giant blue coneflower in a field of dandelions.

Daddy opened the front door of the church and released a furnace blast. There was a center aisle, with about a dozen hard wooden pews on either side, and a potbellied stove near the altar. I wondered if it had a fire going. All the ladies were wearing hats and waving paper fans from a local funeral parlor, while the men stared forward and looked miserable. A scrawny, balding man with round spectacles who surely came into this world in the nineteenth century pounded the lectern with one hand, and shook his Bible with the other. Two elders, right out of American Gothic, sat in high back chairs on the platform behind him, nodding. All three wore black suits, black ties and white shirts. Suddenly, the preacher started in with a chant. I could not understand what he was saying. "Amens" went up all over the place. I felt my mother tighten on my right, and I stood on the pew, Daddy on my left, hypnotized and horrified all at once, wondering what was going to happen next. I had my arm around his neck, and looked quickly at him, since he seemed to be jiggling. He was hiding a smile. (To this day, Daddy can work up an imitation of that preacher bleating, and nothing tickles him more. I saw my grandfather whack him on the leg with his cane more than once for doing it, when Daddy must have been at least forty.) Daddy's take on the situation did nothing to relieve me. I was scared, and I wanted to be back at my church, comfortable, with my cousins and friends and the preacher whose voice would lull me to sleep with my head in Mama's lap as she stroked my hair.

• • •

Mama rarely made us do something we truly did not want to do, but the one area that left no room for negotiation, the place where my tiny little mother became Napoleon, was church attendance. The mere suggestion of staying home on Sunday morning brought on Guilt Armageddon: *After all God does for you, you can give him a couple of hours a week? The Devil is after you! I raised you better than that. Every time you miss makes the next time easier. What has gotten into you?*

Mama knew how scared I was at Sandy Grove Primitive Baptist that day. She still laughs at how vividly I can recall that afternoon, and she loves to talk about the time she was scared at a church.

She grew up in the 1940s in a tiny farm community and her family went to the Southern Baptist church less than a half mile down the road. But just on the other side of her parents' tobacco field was a Holy Roller church, about the size of a large storage building. They held services at night sometimes, and she and her sisters and brother could often hear the congregants having a big time. They wanted to see what went on behind those frosted glass windows. One spring evening, they couldn't stand it anymore. Risking the wrath of my grandmother, they slipped out of the house, across the field and into the back of the church.

To hear Mama describe it—and she would never use these words—all Hell was breaking loose. The first thing the siblings saw was a healing, which involved the preacher "speaking in tongues," and then smacking two or three folks right in the middle of the forehead, so hard they had to be caught and laid out by other congregants. There was music, and chanting and hollering and carrying-on. And then, in the middle of the chaos, hands went into a wooden box and snakes were brought into the mix. As the reptiles were waved and faiths about to be tested, one boy got a running start and jumped out of an open window near the front of the church, diving through cleanly while never breaking stride.

That was enough for the curiosity-seeking Batchelor children. They bolted out of the door they came in, running full speed across the pitch-black field and not stopping until they reached the safety of their house.

Mama said Granny never mentioned the disobedience, figuring the fright was lesson enough to mind your mama next time.

• • •

I went to Sunday School and Vacation Bible School, learned the Ten Commandments and other verses, said my prayers before bed, said the blessing before every meal (Mama said if you didn't, the food strengthened the Devil), and paid attention to the role models in my community. They were leaders, they had peace, they had confidence and they all credited God for the blessings in their lives.

At eight, I convinced Mama to let me talk to the new pastor, the first one we'd had whose sermon I didn't sleep through every Sunday. He asked me questions to see if I understood what I was asking: I wanted to be baptized. I had come to a decision of heart and mind and conscience, that Jesus had died for me and offered salvation. For all her insistence on church attendance, Mama took a big step back on the matter of being born again. This was something I had to do on my own, and then I had to walk the aisle by myself, to make public my decision and affirm it was mine alone. Coercion would have been a sin in its own category.

A couple of weeks later, on a cold February night, I stepped down into the warm, comforting waters of the baptismal pool in the old wooden church. I stood on two stacked cinder blocks so my head would be above the water, and grasped the preacher's robed arm with both of my hands. As the congregation looked on, Reverend Jenkins said some words, most of which I don't remember, until the last part: *"And raised again in the newness of life."* I went under and came back up quickly, feeling the cool air as it braced my skin. After I changed clothes, I stood at the front of the church with the pastor and an adult who had also been baptized, and we accepted hugs and encouragement until I thought my legs would give out.

• • •

As I moved through college and young adulthood, I started to tire of religion. Not Christianity, but rigidity. We had changed pastors a couple of times, and frankly, services were boring. We were doing the same things, in the same order, the same way, because we had always done them that way. We did little to draw and retain new, young members. I looked around one day and realized that I was the only person from my high school graduating class who still attended my church, and for a couple of years, my wife Kristi and I were the only twenty-somethings in the congregation. Had church become irrelevant? Or had the message become centered on guilt and inadequacy? Was it just boring? The storms that were rocking churches everywhere were not going to just go around ours; a certain element considered the place a club, one that had been plenty successful and had no reason to change.

Just as we were finding ourselves struggling to stay awake physically and spiritually, a childhood buddy, the son of one of our most energetic former pastors, came back to our church as youth minister. His experience was broader. God was not about having to dress up and be bored. Worship time was something to enjoy, not dread.

It was just what Kristi and I needed. My view of church shifted from a stiff, inflexible, set of rules (religion) to something altogether different—having a relationship with God, being thankful and loving others.

• • •

We had plenty of blessings to count. Out of nowhere, an opportunity to own a photography and custom framing business and run it together fell in place and worked for eighteen years. When we prayed and stopped thinking about things we wanted, or getting ahead, our blessings increased. When it looked like we might never have children, we were blessed with three.

But even for the faithful, Christianity is not an unending gravy train of gifts. Jesus is not Santa Claus. We had two miscarriages; we lost family members. Economic challenges swamped our business. We lost some of our closeness.

Out of all of these things, we learned the value of questioning our faith. I never did this growing up; it would have been unheard of to think about such things as, *Why do I believe what I believe? Is it real? How do I know there is a God?*

The questions became more pronounced as my world got turned on its ear. I pondered a career change and went to graduate school where I met people who not only had no exposure to church, they aggressively challenged the faith that was part of me.

Once so sure of myself and where I stood, I was on shaky ground. I was travelling a lonely road in pursuit of a tenure track job as an English professor: a Christian, mostly conservative, in a field dominated by liberal, non-Christians. This was a really good thing. I realized that in many ways, when I emerged from those cleansing waters as a third-grader, I had put my faith on autopilot. I had broken the rudder on my life and was just making small, unending circles that led nowhere.

• • •

I was sure I would be self-employed and continue to run my studio until retirement. We had investments that were not huge, but they were growing. We were coming off our best year of gross sales ever. We had healthy children. Faith came easy.

But then, the image started to get wrinkles. A deadbeat tenant almost cost me my rental property which we had purchased in better times, and the business took a nosedive. For the first time, creditors were being put off, stacked in a queue, and meeting monthly obligations—even with our modest lifestyle—became a challenge as my income was trimmed by a quarter, then half, then three quarters. The dream of being debt free by the time our oldest got to college gave way to questions like, Can pay the mortgage if we put off the car payment, or the credit card or the cell phone bills? We even had to drop our health insurance.

I'd be lying if I didn't admit the thoughts that lurked in the shadows of my mind: "God, why are you letting this happen to me?" But they never made it to my heart. All of the things that had been turned on their head were decisions I made without consultation or request for guidance. Prayer became secondary to opportunity.

It took being on the brink of financial and emotional collapse to finally let go of the rudder again and say, "Here is everything, it is on the table. I'm all in, my faith is pushed to the middle, and I'm waiting for five new cards. Deal."

• • •

Thirty years after my last visit to Sandy Grove Primitive Baptist Church, I went back. There was no service, as most of the former members have been laid to rest in the cemetery out back. Their descendants have moved on. Mama called, told me that one of the church's neighbors had laid a claim on the property, sometimes known as a squatter's deed, since a living person didn't hold the deed and there were no longer regular meetings. She wanted to go inside one more time. Rumor had it that the neighbor planned to demolish the building, and had stopped attempts for additional members to be buried in the 150-year-old burial ground.

I untied the wire that held the front door shut. The church seemed so much smaller than I remembered. The pot-bellied stove was gone, but the pipe dangled from the ceiling. There were bits of wood and debris from ceiling leaks and damage, but all of the pews were in place just as they had been for the last service. Where they had felt hard and uncomfortable to me as a child, they now seemed solid and well built. Even from the back row, it seemed like I could reach out and touch the pulpit, which still sat in its place. Abandoned, the church was far less scary than it had been when I was child: light flooded in from the beautiful, tall windows on the side, beams revealed by the circulating dust. This building, once filled with churchgoers, intimidating and frightening and hot so many years ago, now offered a peaceful sanctuary of solitude and communion.

We walked around for a few minutes, not saying much of anything. I sat by a window and offered a short prayer. In a building with an unsure future, I asked for guidance and reassurance about my own days to come, for comfort, for strength. I took the warmth of the sun as it pushed through the thin, distorted, antique windows as my answer. I would have to take my next steps on faith alone, into the dark unknown, trusting that God had answers better than mine, could see where I could not.

I went back to Sandy Grove a few weeks later, and along with some other folks, loaded up a pew for me, and one for my parents. Mine sits on my front porch.

Not long after that, with no legal documents or right, the neighbor rented a bulldozer, pushed over one of the oldest structures in the county, covered it with gasoline, and within hours reduced it to ashes. Just like that, something sure and solid and constant became nothing more than a memory.

• • •

I've made that career transition, and while my faith was stretched to its limit, it did not prove to be brittle, but tough and elastic, holding in place. It was not easy to let go of the business, one we had built and assumed would last a working lifetime. But it had become a stronghold, a master to be served. As hard as it was to close the doors that last time, it was also a release. As solid as the studio had been, pursuing writing and teaching seems to be a more true fit, a circuitous route to where I should be, a homecoming.

Now, on cool weekend afternoons in the fall, I sometimes like to go sit on my pew with my banjo or my guitar and pick a few bluegrass standards. The century-old oak is solid and sturdy and stable. I pulled that long bench out of the place where it had been and grown accustomed, giving it a new purpose and saving it from being consumed in flames. That pew and I have a lot in common.

• • •

Purchase other Black Rose Writing titles at www.blackrosewriting.com/books
and use promo code PRINT to receive a 20% discount.

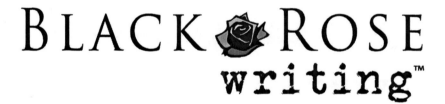

CPSIA information can be obtained at www.ICGtesting.com
Printed in the USA
LVOW10s1338240915

455574LV00019B/683/P

9 781612 965369